## Praise for Maralys Wills

As I read, each sentence compelled me to read the next, and before long I was completely lost in your wonderful book.

—SIDNEY SHELDON
Author, *The Other Side of Midnight, Master of the Game, Rage of Angels* and *The Sands of Time*

Solid, practical, realistic advice, packed with useful information and examples. Her informal style is inspiring, entertaining, and motivating.

—MARYLIN HUDSON
*Orange Coast* Magazine

Who would believe a how-to book that's a page turner? Maralys Wills pulls it off with a compelling narrative arc that propels a wealth of do-able info for the reader-writer. Building the romantic scene, developing characters, writing the query letter, marketing and more—it's all here in wisdom gleaned from years of writing triumph, and, most important, failure.

It's a realistic book, an honest book that allows readers to learn from each step and misstep, each revision, rejection—and advance check. Best of all, it's an attitude of warmth and encouragement to every writer, from novice to professional.

—BEVERLY BUSH SMITH
Author, *Wings of a Dove, Evidence of Things Unseen* and *Caught in the Middle*

I read *Damn the Rejections* in one sitting — not unusual if this were a novel, but it isn't. It's an instructional book on the art of writing. Rather than a dry treatise covering rules and regulations, it is a series of signposts to steer a would-be author through that deceptively simple minefield called creative writing. The book vibrates with the life and humor of a good memoir and, indeed, it is both a funny story and an excellent guide for storytellers.

— E. ERVIN TIBBS
Author, *Sunset Tomorrow*

With skill and grace, Maralys Wills showed me the power of self-editing. Without her, so many of us might never be published.

— BARBARA BENEDICT
Author, 15 book

Reading just a few lines of Maralys Will's sparkling prose is enough to prove why she is the perfect person to advise others on the principles of writing. However, being unable to stop with those few lines you will be rewarded with a book that entertains while it educates. Having written memoir, thrillers, romance, and how-tos, she covers the gamut of genres and styles. Learning a craft has never been so much fun.

— JAN MURRA
Author, *Castoff*

Maralys Wills created a professional and comfortable atmosphere in her classroom, giving students an opportunity to learn and grow. Criticism was never allowed to be mean spirited. Ms. Wills' writing knowledge went a long way in helping me reach my goals.

— LINDA PRINE
Author, *Lady Rebel*

This is a must read for every writer — both informative and entertaining.

—JERRY D. SIMMONS
Former Time Warner Publishing Executive
and Author, *What Writers Need to Know About Publishing*

When it comes to motivating authors, Maralys Wills certainly knows her subject. Her knowledge as a multi-published author, together with her unique style and ability to teach writing in a way that gets results is a gift few instructors possess. Out of the twenty students enrolled in our class, nineteen have since become published.

—MINDY NEFF
Author, 25 books

Maralys Wills gives you the gift of her experience. She will teach you and inspire you and give you the tools you need to survive the sometimes rough world of publishing.

— MAUREEN CHILD
Author, 88 books

A teacher beyond compare, what Maralys doesn't know about writing, hasn't been written. If you are looking to make the leap from amateur to published writer, then Maralys Wills will take you there.

— SANDY NOVY CHVOSTAL
Author, 9 books

# Damn the Rejections, Full Speed Ahead

## Also by Maralys Wills

*Manbirds: Hang Gliders & Hang Gliding*

*Tempest & Tenderness*

*Mountain Spell*

*A Match for Always*

*Soar and Surrender*

*Fun Games for Great Parties*

*Scatterpath*

*Higher than Eagles*

*Save My Son*

*A Circus without Elephants*

*A Clown in the Trunk*

# Damn the Rejections, Full Speed Ahead

## The Bumpy Road to Getting Published

Maralys Wills

Stephens Press • Las Vegas, Nevada

Ray Newton, Editor
Sue Campbell, Art Director
Stacey Fott, Publishing Coordinator

Cataloging-in-Publication

Wills, Maralys.
   Damn the rejection, full speed ahead : the bumpy road to getting published / Maralys Wills.
   242 p. ; 23 cm.

Relating her own experiences as a writer dealing with rejection by publishers, the author provides advice for aspiring authors, both in the craft of writing and in working with publishers.

ISBN: 1-932173-92-7 (hc)
ISBN-13: 978-1-932173-92-5 (hc)
ISBN: 1-932173-91-9 (pbk.)
ISBN-13: 978-1-932173-91-8 (pbk.)

1. Authors and publishers.  2. Authorship.  I. Title.

808.'02 dc22            2008            2008928397

STEPHENS PRESS, LLC
A Stephens Media Company
Post Office Box 1600
Las Vegas, NV 89125-1600
www.stephenspress.com
Printed in Hong Kong

The highway to "published" is littered with stones
And potholes and dust and authorial bones.
When editors snub me with reasoning spurious
Instead of dismay or descent into furious
A soul-saving litany rings in my head—
*Damn the Rejections, Full Speed Ahead.*

# Acknowledgements

No book of mine has been written without the help and enthusiasm of others. In fact, many others.

Always at the top of the list is my husband, Rob, who makes the whole writing life possible. Let's face it, a woman creates best when pampered by plenty of dinners out and no yard work. Ours is a perfect arrangement: Rob claims he does his finest thinking when I'm upstairs writing—because only then am I not downstairs talking.

Heartfelt thanks goes to reader Susan Hawken, and to members of my critique group, both past and present: Barbara French, Michelle Lack, Bill Wilbur, P.J. Penman, Allene Symons, and Pam Tallman. And to Walt Golden, a special thanks—and he knows what it's for.

Another warm thanks to Erv Tibbs, who read the whole manuscript twice, and whose unflagging enthusiasm through many re-writes kept me going.

I'm truly indebted to long time friend and author Jan Murra, who also read the manuscript twice—and suggested changes that made all the difference.

Thanks to my editor, Carolyn Hayes Uber, who would be any author's idea of a perfect editor: she's full of creative ideas, she makes things happen fast, and she's wholly supportive of my work.

— MW

Chapter One

# Ten thousand Rejections

Nobody gets 10,000 rejections. But to some of us who've been writing a long time, it feels like it.

We think we must have accumulated that many by now, but when you do the math that's a thousand rejections a year for ten years, so of course it couldn't happen. You have to be a normal person to write, and a normal person would put up with two, maybe three years of that nonsense and then he'd light a match and toss his rejections and manuscripts into the bonfire.

So you can't get 10,000. But one thousand? Well . . . one thousand is possible, and if I had the time I might count my thirty-years' worth and see how close I've come. Like most writers, I've saved them, every last demeaning impersonal form-letter refusal, with that masochistic attitude that partly defines us. If we weren't into outrunning fires and swimming through floods, we wouldn't be writers. We've got something to prove, we authors. We know publication comes hard, and we want our non-writing friends and everyone else to know it's hard, so there's a kind of unspoken contest in the writing underworld, me pitting my rejection slips against your rejection slips. Then, when publication happens, it's such a spectacular achievement.

Sooner or later, though, a writer who loves tinkering with words and can't be dissuaded, has to stop focusing on negatives and begin pushing ahead with the strategies that work. In the end, getting published becomes a matter of attitude. As I tell my students, the whole publishing game is attitude; it's attitude as you write, and later when you're trying to sell. It's attitude every time you rip apart your own work, hoping to make it stop humming and actually sing. It's attitude that makes you declare: *Damn the rejections, full speed ahead.*

THIS BOOK IS TWO things: it's a writing book with concrete, very specific chapters devoted to the craft of writing—tips drawn from 21 years of teaching novel-writing to college students who happen to be adults.

It's also a book about my personal journey from 127 separate rejections (yes, I counted them), to a few published articles, and eventually to the sale of twelve books—and one in particular, the Book of My Heart. All my students, in fact every writer I've ever worked with, has a Book of the Heart. When you finally sell that neglected manuscript whose pulse has always been in perfect sync with your own, it's the ultimate triumph.

My journey, though, is not typical, it hasn't followed any normal, published-author pattern. Instead, I've been on a deviant path that I wouldn't recommend to any beginning writer (though it's worked for me), a trail that's wandered through so many different styles of writing and visited such a variety of publishing houses, that for years I've called myself a genre hopper.

Well, you have to call yourself something.

When people ask, "What kind of books do you write?" there's always a split second of silence. Finally I say, "All kinds. I'm a genre hopper," and people look startled and half don't know what a genre is, so I try to explain, and soon we're discussing books and categories and my unwanted propensity to see every aspect of life as a story.

The truth is, I never chose to become a genre hopper, never pictured myself turning out such an eclectic mix of books, all in unrelated categories. Among my many writing fantasies there was never an image of me pitching my tent in the romance camp, or the memoir camp, or any other camp. I just wanted to write.

From the viewpoint of publishers, it's all been a terrible mistake. Famous writers simply don't do what I've done—zoomed about like a drunken honeybee in and out of half a dozen writing categories. Publishers know how the game works best; they know how careers are built. They expect you to choose a genre before you're eleven and stick to it until you're old enough for a coronary bypass.

They're right, of course. What was I seeking . . . obscurity?

But here's the But, and you knew it was coming. I've had a wonderful time writing those twelve books. Thanks to having published in six distinct categories, I've absorbed a variety of writing lessons and, like autumn leaves gathered along the route, they stand out in memory, each leaf significant, each lesson a gift for my students.

Above all, I'm leading a life I adore, not only writing but teaching others, trying my best to inspire, illuminate, and unravel the mysteries of this zen-like craft.

I'm not famous and I'm not rich, but those are the only drawbacks. The rest has been downright wonderful.

What follows, then, are some truisms, some personal stories, that will, optimistically, apply to many writers in a variety of fields.

READING, OF COURSE, IS rather like the tiny cork ball in the heart of a baseball—you can't have the baseball without the cork. For most of us, reading is where the writing game starts. The universe was created with a bang—and then there were books . . .

Like other writers, I'd always been one of those kids who'd read **anything**—whatever was lying around on the coffee table or couch, or whatever books I could steal from my mother's shelves. I surreptitiously devoured dozens of hers—*They Came to a River*, *Our Hearts Were Young and Gay* while quietly sniffling over mine—the crying books like *Bambi* and *Heidi*, or the thinking books like *Alice in Wonderland*, and *Winnie the Pooh*, most having arrived at my door as though by magic, mailed to me by distant relatives. At breakfast I read the backs of cereal boxes.

Whenever life was unexciting, which was most of the time growing up on an isolated ranch in Northern California, I'd escape from the tedium by reading. If my mother told me to go clean the upstairs bathroom, I'd disappear for an hour ... most of it spent sitting on the potty with my latest book, and a few minutes at the end with the can of cleanser. "What are you *doing?*" she'd shout up the stairs, and I'd shout back, "Just finishing, Mom, just finishing," which meant I'd finally start scrubbing.

Boding poorly for my mathematical future, I even fled fourth-grade long division by disappearing into books. There was always some volume or other in the cubby of my desk, and during the dullest forms of math which, it seemed to me at the time included math of every description, I left the nothingness of numbers by sneaking the book onto my lap. Surely not an act to be proud of, and even today when it comes to figures I'm inclined not to be properly concerned about one zero more or less. There was the time I was supposed to send my son $600 and absently wrote the check for $6,000.

Today, when I speak to school children, I try to share this spirit of obsessive reading. I always lean closer to the group, sitting tuck-legged on the auditorium floor, and ask with a conspiratorial smile, "How many of you read books when you're not supposed to? How many of you are *sneak* readers?" When the hands go up I nod and say, "*You are the flashlight and blanket readers—the real readers!*"

THE RANCH THAT TURNED me into a fanatical reader was 320 acres of pine, cedar, fir, and spruce trees, a richly-hued forest near California's isolated and majestic Mount Shasta. My mother, who carted me, and my younger brother Allan to the boonies, was a bit of a nut bent on escaping her rich, tyrannical father. She was about to introduce us to a Swiss skier, her third husband (out of seven).

"You'll love this ranch, Kiddies," she told Allan and me as we drove North from Los Angeles. It was her first mention of exactly where we were headed (we were nine and seven), and right away I began musing about clothes-to-be-a-rancher-in. "You'll have to forgive the house. It's old and cranky and really not livable—at least not yet. But," she added with the usual gaiety in her voice, "we'll have a great time. For the first summer we'll all be living in tents."

Tents?

"You know . . . outside under the trees. You see, the house doesn't have any bathrooms."

No bathrooms?

"And we'll have to use kerosene lanterns for light. The place has no electricity."

No electricity?

"But don't worry," she said, seeing the surprise on our faces. " We'll soon have bathrooms installed in the house. Trust me, Kiddies." She threw us one of her big, delicious laughs. "It'll be an adventure. You'll love it. And I plan to have the house renovated. We'll be living there by late fall. Long before the snow starts."

Snow?

It was all so startling, yet somehow exciting, tripping off the lips of my gregarious, fun-loving mother. My mental wardrobe kept changing as she talked. Farming. Camping. Snow. How **did** one dress for all that?

Neither Allan nor I noticed that she had made no promises about electricity, a commodity we'd always taken for granted. We'd started our lives in the city, where light simply came with a click or a twist. Kerosene lanterns sounded like . . . well, I couldn't picture what they'd be like. I certainly never imagined I'd do all my future nighttime reading, right up until high school, by kerosene lantern.

But then I never would have guessed that reading was about **all** I'd find on the ranch to do. The trees that framed the ranch house like a beautifully-matted picture were inspiring . . . so lush, so many-hued in their pine, fir and cedar greenness that any random grouping could almost make you weep.

But trees were not people. You couldn't talk to trees, couldn't play games with them. Our nearest neighbors were a mile away, a family I mostly felt sorry for, consisting of the struggling, impoverished parents, and their three overworked boys—and beyond them was nobody and six more neighborless miles to town. So most of the time there was only Allan to play with.

Allan was fairly decent for a brother, but he beat me so many times at Monopoly I came to detest the game. Even when he loaned me money and forgave the rent when I landed on his rotten, overdeveloped

Park Place I couldn't enjoy it, knowing it was only Allan's largesse that kept me alive.

Fierce competitor that I was, even at nine, I longed to best him at the game. But somehow I never did. In my heart of hearts, I knew it wasn't all luck.

Unable to beat Allan, I reverted to reading books.

One day I decided I would also write, and having no paper available, I carefully ripped out the early blank pages in half a dozen classy adult books, tied them together with string, scribbled a few sentences on each page—which amounted to a wispy, breathy story—and presented it to my mother. "I've written a book," I said.

She glanced at my crude little pages and smiled. "That's nice, dear." This, before she discovered the source of those blank pages.

That dismissive smile: you might say Mom was my first editor.

OUR MOTHER HAD GONE TO Smith College and become a woman of contradictions. Her hearty laugh, perpetual zaniness, and predilection for trying out new husbands, belied a delicately sketched inner person left over from Smith, a mostly-hidden persona that was pure intellectual snob. Privately, out of hearing of the ranch hands, she told Allan and me, "You will go to college and you will *be somebody*. You will rise above this town. You will be *educated*." She may have worn blue jeans and Western, alabaster-buttoned shirts, but her real identity lay with her den and a wall that was covered floor to ceiling in books. She had everything from Kahlil Gibran to *Cheaper by the Dozen,* whose author she knew personally because they were classmates at Smith.

If Mom ever noticed that her daughter was raiding those bookshelves, she never mentioned it. Our mother drifted in and out of her role as parent, at times careless, often unobservant. And just as carelessly I pictured myself writing like all those mixed voices had done before me.

IN LATER YEARS, AS I was bounding from one kind of book to the next, writing madly on whatever subject seemed fascinating at the moment (and far too many subjects intrigued me then and do now and most appear book-worthy), I learned an awful truth: the publishing world isn't crazy about genre hoppers.

It wasn't a truth that fit even slightly with what I was doing.

From everywhere came the same stern message: *Serious Writers stick to one genre.* And best-selling authors *really* stick to one genre.

Of course. Successful publishing is all built on name recognition—on a reader's expectation that if he buys a book by Robin Cook it will indeed be a medical thriller and not a Western a la Louis L'Amour.

Publishers want their writers' names to appear in crossword puzzles, as in "Medical writer, Cook."

Most editors would say what I, as a writing teacher for lo these many years, have said over and over: find your niche and stick with it, polish your words until they shine, challenge your genre, push back the boundaries, but stay in one category until you're brilliant . . . until you become the John Grisham of your field and your name is found in crossword puzzles.

So WHAT DO I have to offer, me, a genre-hopping cricket who's broken all the career rules and a few more besides?

Well, I suppose three things: an analytical look at the quirks that separate and define different genres (God knows, I had to glean them all myself, one by one) . . . some writing principles that kept appearing and re-appearing like stubborn mantras during my 21 years of teaching . . . and Attitude.

As I jumped from non-fiction, to romance, to how-to, to techno-thriller, to memoir, to public policy, to humor, it came to me the hard way that not all genres are created equal. Writing styles vary from one to another. Mood is different. The cadence, the "swing" of a book is different. And certainly readers' expectations are different.

Usually I learned these differences at the wrong end of the spectrum—after I'd finished the entire book, after I'd typed "The End." I never learned **any** of my lessons before I started.

As a writing teacher, I now have an abiding interest in saving other writers time, in helping them learn early some of what they need to know before they plunge into a genre. And with this comes a burning desire to point out the writing goofs I see over and over, the trip wires that snag so many of my students and fling the very pens from their fingers.

But the best of what I can offer is Attitude.

Attitude is what makes you send a book out ten, twenty, thirty times, and then, when it keeps returning like a demented boomerang and it's so untouched it's obviously never been read, or it's so mangled somebody ate their dinner on it, you rip into the book and polish and upgrade every sentence you can, and finally send it out again . . . ten, twenty, thirty more times.

Attitude is what makes you go out as a virgin author more times than anyone could possibly be a virgin, knowing your name will ring no bells, that you will still be "Maralys . . . Who?" to every agent or editor who glances at the title page.

Attitude is what makes you get out of bed at three a.m. (as I did this morning), and jot down the reasons that just came to you about why a chapter might be drooping like a dying lily.

Attitude is the reason—the whole reason—that a genre-hopper with zero name recognition ever sells twelve books.

Has it been worth it?

Well . . . just ask my students.

THE NEXT CHAPTER COVERS critique groups, an important place to start in one's quest to become a serious writer. Critique groups are one of the few ways an aspiring writer can get meaningful, hands-on help with his work. For me they've been vital, no matter what my current genre.

## Chapter Two

# CRITIQUE GROUPS
# (AND OTHER WAYS TO SAVE TIME)

SONDRA BAKER MILLS HAD a father who beat her when he ran out of patience and ignored her the rest of the time, and a mother who baked delicious cookies and seemed to love her oldest daughter ... but not well enough, apparently, because the mother deserted the family when Sondra was only twelve. Which makes Sondra a typical writer.

All writers have terrible childhoods. Without a terrible childhood you grow up with nothing special to write about, and you have to wait for material to come along ... maybe until you've suffered through a miserable young adulthood.

New to my class but a writer for three years, Sondra handed me a longish piece about her life. "It's just sitting there looking at me," she said with a smile, "it's shivering and I think it may be sick, but I can't tell for sure." She added, "My aunt loves it. But my friends ... they probably don't. Friends don't tell you the truth, do they?" It was a rhetorical question, requiring no response.

No, I thought, they don't. But how can they? They're friends. I smiled. "Non-writers seldom know what to say."

I added her piece to the other class submissions. We'd be critiquing it soon.

"I sent it out to four editors," she said as an afterthought.

"What did they say?"

She shrugged. "I haven't heard back. I guess I never will. It's been a year."

She sat down in the front row and watched me expectantly, a puppy waiting to learn new tricks, her hope as plain as a bare light bulb. Writers may have terrible childhoods, may once have wallowed in misery, but somehow they emerge as optimists.

I thought, *Every writer I know is an optimist. Whatever angst they convey on paper, the process of finding the words demands confidence—and yes, optimism.*

My belief in writer-optimism governs my teaching life down to the last sentence I scribble on student manuscripts. It is my job to buoy up my writers, to keep them floating on a kind of invisible raft that gets punctured occasionally but never quite deflates. The day I push one of them under, he will stop writing. I've seen it happen in other classes. You drown 'em, you lose 'em.

So now Sondra Mills had found a writing class. There, with luck, she would finally get the line-by-line analysis, the fine-tuning of her work that simply can't be found anywhere else.

And sooner or later, if she cared enough, she'd join a critique group.

And that's the point of this chapter: what to expect from critique groups. Which we'll get to in a minute. But first, why does anyone need them?


YEARS AGO, WHEN ONE of my students became exasperated with the class, he said in a flip tone, "I'll send my book out and let an editor fix it."

I tried not to laugh. But of course he didn't know, as new writers don't, that publishing is heartless and editors may read but they seldom fix. And the news gets worse.

No professional will spend more than a couple of minutes on a piece he considers amateurish, and hardly longer on a work that's merely adequate. Agents and editors, universally, are swamped—buried in submissions, limited in reading time—so they're forced to make snap judgments, most of which are encompassed by the word No.

So where, besides classes and critique groups, can you learn how to write?

You learn from endless reading, of course. And trying to do it. With enough time, I suppose one can learn to write with no help at all, just by writing, and throwing away and writing again . . . by practicing for years and years, as did some of the old, great Russian masters.

But that's not how today's writers learn.

When aspiring authors finally realize (as I did), that learning by oneself is like surgery self-taught and might take eighty years and kill you in the bargain, they seek out excellent teachers. And when they get a little bit good, they learn even more from critique groups formed out of writing classes.

Sometimes you can join a group that's already established; other times you have to look around at your fellow students and form your own group. I've done it both ways.

A CRITIQUE GROUP YOU can trust is your test market. It's the place to show your work and find out just what *is* wrong with that limp-wristed paragraph. It's the place where people will tell you honestly that a chapter isn't "working." It should also be the place where people write "good," "nice," or occasionally "great" next to passages they like.

The critiquing rules that govern my novel-writing class belong in most critique groups as well:

1. Critiques should be positive. Readers should actively seek out and note the good word, line or paragraph—remembering that writers learn as much from what they're doing right as what they're doing wrong.

2. Critiques should be specific . . . "Here's where the character gets unlikable." Or, "Your character wouldn't say 'Go ahead, be honest about my faults,' when he's so arrogant that he's never accepted criticism in his life."

I once belonged to a critique group where a fellow writer's inevitable comment was, "The tone isn't right." Just that, the tone wasn't right, and since he never gave examples, or suggested how we might move our work up or down the tonal scale, none of us knew *what,* exactly, he was referring to. Mainly, his critiques were useless. After awhile, we'd hear him start with the "tone" bit, and the rest of us would glance at each other and shrug. And indeed, over the years, his vague assessments never helped anybody. But since he was published and the rest of us weren't—and since we weren't there to critique our critquers—we all just learned to ignore him.

3. Whenever possible, concrete suggestions for improvements should be offered . . . tips based on the writing class you've all taken together.

4. Any group dominated by a shark should be disbanded. Preferably, you should kill the shark on your way out.

Nothing will stifle creativity faster than the critiquer who's "out to get" other writers. Subtly, or not so subtly, a shark is so impossible to please that other authors become frustrated, then discouraged, and finally defeated. I know of a critique group dominated by a lady shark—a regular female Jaws—who so dispirited a fellow writer that the woman's self-esteem plummeted and she quit working on her very touching memoir for three years.

Critique groups can be organized in two ways, and both are effective. A. Members read the submissions at home and bring them back to discuss. B. Submissions are read aloud at each meeting. (Preferably not by the writer, who can, by inflection and dramatic presentation, lay an all-too-attractive slant on her work.)

Either way, each member should have a copy of the material so notes can be jotted in the margins. It's hard to hang on to each and every thought when a whole chapter is presented orally.

Advantages go with both methods. The read-at-home material gets a thorough going-over, often line-by-line. On the other hand, an author receives a distinct impression from hearing his work read aloud. He senses when something goes on too long, he can literally hear it bogging down. Many a time I've listened to my own words and thought, Oh quick, get past that page and on to the good stuff. Obviously, that page needed trimming. Believe it or not, I can sometimes assess the effect of my words by how the other members are breathing . . . or moving. I'm just grateful I've never heard anyone snoring.

Groups can meet once a week or every two weeks, or maybe once a month. If everyone is actively writing, five members is an ideal number—at least it's been so for us. More than that, and it's hard to get read each time. Submissions tend to consist of a double-spaced chapter, ten to fifteen manuscript pages—to match the ever-shorter chapters in today's books—which in turn parallel readers' ever shorter attention spans.

THE TRICKIEST ASPECT OF working with a critique group is assessing the critiques . . . deciding how much weight to give each opinion. Sometimes, in read-aloud groups, the members fall into line like lemmings behind the strongest-minded critiquer and they all go marching off together echoing each other's comments, and the writer wonders whether each of them would have come up with the same impression separately.

Clearly there's an advantage to read-at-home submissions, where, when several people note the same problem, it must be taken seriously. Occasionally, one person-—and only one—sees something so important you wonder how everyone else missed it.

The second-trickiest aspect is having the guts to trust your own judgment. But you must. You absolutely must believe that you are the final arbiter of what's good in your own manuscript . . . or even in somebody's else's. Which seems to contradict everything said so far.

If ever I saw that principle in action, it jumped out at me early in one of my critique groups. Here was a group of fairly smart writers who took each other's submissions home each week and brought them back later to discuss.

But I had a problem with one of our members: her chapters were always so good I could never find anything to criticize. I loved what she wrote, nearly every word. I'd read her golden prose and think, *How can anyone criticize this? What can they possibly say?* And I'd feel somehow inadequate, knowing that one way or another my fellow critiquers would find flaws I didn't see and pick away at this lovely work, while I, alone among the pack, would once again find nothing to offer but compliments.

Sure enough, each week, the others ripped and tore and nit-picked to death the work I found so nearly perfect . . . and all the time I was thinking, *You guys must be desperate to flaunt your hatchets. None of you are as good as she is.* Finally the writer quit our group in disgust. And then, for other reasons, so did I.

Obviously that wasn't a useful or supportive group, and the two of us were right to leave. For a couple of years I was quietly glad I'd trusted my own judgment and said what I believed to be true instead of being swept into fault-finding for its own sake. Scenes from her perfectly-written chapters lingered in my memory.

And then it happened: our local writer proved her detractors wrong and became a best-selling author. Though we'd all known her by a different name, the world recognizes her today as Elizabeth George.

FOR THE SUGGESTIBLE AND perhaps too-submissive author, there's a hidden danger in working with even the best critique groups—namely, trying to incorporate every change that's offered by someone else. First, that kind of re-writing is impossible; on any given passage, diverse readers will have diverse viewpoints. And second, by attempting to use the input of too great a variety of readers, the writer's own vision of her work is lost. As one of my excellent writing students says, "If I listen to too many critiques, my work turns into mush."

An even worse fate befalls the insecure writer who feels she cannot move on until *everyone* approves of her work. Which, of course, will never happen. If you revise your work a hundred times and submit it to others a hundred times, each of those times readers will find passages to criticize.

A member of one of my earliest critique groups did exactly that— kept reworking her first chapter and re-submitting it, always hoping for perfect marks and permission to move on. She never achieved perfection, of course, and so she never felt she could write a second chapter. Three years later that hapless woman had moved to another group, and from what I heard was still re-working her first chapter.

Eventually, and sooner rather than later, the writer must say, " This is as good as I can make it, and on we go to the next chapter."

And here might be a good place to record the ultimate in strange critiques. One of my students once had a woman tell him his work was 'feathery.' "I looked at her," he said, "and I guess I hurt her feelings, because I said, 'What the hell does *that* mean?'"

HAVING PARTICIPATED IN A number of critique groups, one for almost twenty years, I've developed ways of wringing maximum benefit from all those clever minds.

If someone writes a "great" on any line of mine, I keep it no matter what. The other comments I think about carefully, trying to see my work as the observer saw it.

The truth is, I **always** pay attention to critiques. I listen hard, ponder intently . . . try on changes for fit.

*And then I go on and do what's best for the manuscript.* Some comments miss the point of the piece. Others offer changes that "stick out," like a pebble in your shoe.

And then there are those few that suggest a word or line that's absolutely perfect.

At best, every critique makes me take yet another analytical stab at what I've written, to reconsider my words, to try a new slant. Whether I use a given suggestion or not, I nearly always find a way to make the passage brighter, more intelligent, more vivid.

The final result of submitting work to a critique group is that, one way or another, the manuscript ends up better than it was. Which should be the final and only reason for going that route.

After twelve published books, I'm still a slave to my group, meaning I wouldn't dream of sending my agent un-critiqued, first-draft material.

WHAT ABOUT THE SUCCESSFUL authors who've never joined a critique group, think they're a horrible waste of time, and wonder in exclamation points why any writer would submit to such a mauling?

Fair enough. Not everyone needs a group. But it's my contention that every good author has *somebody* who reads his stuff. A wife or husband. An agent. A teacher. A good friend. Somebody. (Grisham mentions his wife—more critical than any editor, he says.)

If there's some brilliant writer out there whose work gets published with no critiquing at all, even from his editor . . . well, frankly, I don't believe such a person exists.

## Chapter Three

# A Forest Fire is Only a Fire

WHEN YOU'RE AN AUTHOR, almost of all life is about writing.

Years ago, I pictured myself as the only survivor in a plane crash, for the stupidest of reasons: I imagined my first-person account would make such a gripping tale it would sell madly, like a book touted by Oprah. Now, with more sense, I've decided that no stampede of buyers could possibly be worth those moments of excruciating, stark terror. . . .

So while we writers certainly don't choose our miserable childhoods, nor do most of us seek out unbearable or life-threatening experiences (except for reporters embedded with combat troops), when they happen to us, we use them.

In his book on writing, Stephen King described at length the disaster that befell him when he was hit by a car while he was out jogging. And for years I wrote stories about the scariest event I lived through as a child. I imagined I had a complete, rounded tale.

I was wrong.

ONLY A YEAR AFTER Allan and I moved to our new ranch, a malignant forest fire swept down from the peaks of Mount Eddy and began eating up our forest in fiery gulps.

The fire was the first truly dramatic thing that ever happened to me. I was ten and wide-eyed, soaking up impressions like a tremulous Bambi, aware of every startling detail—the way, for instance, sparks from the burning trees drifted high in the air and glowed like fireflies.

The process of squirreling away literary nuts to dig up for later use was just starting.

Had he not been away at camp, Allan would have seen how innocently the calamity began . . . the typical hot July morning, a hired hand casually pointing at the sky, a few of us staring upward until we spotted a small puff of white hovering above distant Mount Eddy. I remember being surprised by the look of alarm on the face of my handsome stepfather, Hans.

The smoke—if one could call it that—was just a snowflake of a thing, barely visible, yet here he was, racing for his pickup truck and shouting back at me, "Someone has to tell the Forest Service. Get in, Maralys, we're going to town." Along with everything else we didn't have, we didn't have a phone.

Hans stopped the truck at our neighbors' house. He and the mother, Alice Deetz, exchanged a few anxious words, and with that I jumped out. "I'll just stay here," I said.

He waved and drove away.

In retrospect, Time is unreliable. It telescopes or magnifies until, at dramatic moments, one loses the real sense of it. In only minutes, it seemed, the sky had darkened, and Alice Deetz and her three boys and I were watching flames peek, like Kilroy, over the top of a nearby hill. "There!" someone cried. "Oh! Another one!" A flash of red here. Another there. Then momentarily nothing.

Across the broad meadow from the Deetz's little house, the sharp rise that captured our attention was forested with stately pines, now strangely backlit. Suddenly one of the trees near the ridge ignited like a Roman candle. We all gasped in unison. A steep climb of flame, a bright, upward sparking, and the tree was consumed.

All too soon another tree flamed up. Then a few more. A swarm of fireflies winked across the hill.

Time telescoped with a fury. Within minutes the whole hillside came alive like the sky over Disneyland, sparking, bursting, popping, streaking. I was mesmerized, trembling with nervous excitement. How could this have happened so fast? A short time earlier I'd seen only that bit of cotton fluff in the sky, a city girl assessing the danger as nothing, really nothing, and clearly miles away. And now this!

In stunned fascination the three boys and Alice and I stared at their hill, felt a hot July wind come up and brush our arms, smelled the acrid smoke, surprised that it burned our nostrils.

Overhead, blackened twigs flew by like startled birds, each trailing smoke. Suddenly eight-year-old Jimmy Deetz yelled, "Fire!" and he began running. On the other side of us, across the dirt road near which we stood, tiny flames began to sizzle and pop in the grass. Jimmy Deetz stamped them out with his shoes. His younger brother, Laddie, grabbed a shovel and attacked a small burning shrub until it turned black and smoldering.

I stared in horror.

Still a third shrub ignited and Jimmy ran over, a farm boy long accustomed to working like a man.

I thought, Oh, God. Oh, God. They'll never keep up. The twigs will fly over our heads like winged matches and more fires will start. And sure enough, flames erupted in half a dozen places, and I thought, Even the Deetz boys can't beat back a forest fire.

Hovering near Charlie, the oldest, who was my age and gentler than his brothers, I stood rooted.

Panic welled inside and I wanted to run . . . but where? The reality was horrible, all too obvious. We were surrounded. Flames on the left, flames on the right, and we were in the middle. We were all going to burn. I was sure we would die.

I whimpered and cried. I was a mess.

Charlie, too, was scared and useless.

Joining her two younger sons, Alice Deetz began fighting the small fires, beating at them with the only object at hand, an old broom long discarded outside, with hardly any bristles.

I'd always known Alice had guts. But now she seemed to have no sense. Why are you doing this? I thought. Why? Without knowing the word futility, I understood the concept perfectly.

Just then one of the hired hands came careening down the road from our ranch and I virtually leaped at him, stopping his truck, begging to be taken away. The man shouted at Alice and her boys. "You want to come along?"

"No," said Alice, waving him off. "We'll stay here and fight." Just like they've always done, I thought. Fighting poverty, fighting fire. Never knowing when to give up.

The hired hand swept up Charlie and me and went on. Our self-ishness was monumental and not to be forgiven. Even ten-year-olds should worry about others, but the two of us were like prairie dogs pursued by a hawk, racing for our own burrows and hardly aware of the other dogs. As we tore down the dirt road, I knew only relief that Charlie and I and the driver were outrunning the fire. We were going to live.

THE FIRE COULD NOT have impressed me more. Years later I tried to use the blaze in college English assignments, in creative writing classes. I may have described it well, but I didn't necessarily get "A"s.

Only in retrospect do I realize the forest fire became my first real writing lesson. All I'd managed to do, in those early writing attempts, was create a "slice of life." At the time, I thought I'd written a story.

I hadn't. A slice of life is not a story. It's just a fragment. An isolated happening without purpose or meaning. It doesn't come to anything or "wind up."

"Slice of life," to a writing teacher, is a dirty word . . . make that a dirty phrase. It leaves the reader with too many questions:

So?

What happened next?

How did the characters change?

What's the point?

Eventually I learned that to classify as a story, the tale must have an **ending**. It needs a purpose or theme, too, but it absolutely must have an ending. By the final paragraph, something or someone must have changed. The people involved should be different in some way . . . in attitude, behavior, or with a heightened sense of irony. (A story, by the way, is not an exact duplicate of real life, but merely a gilded imitation called Art.)

For me, finding meaning and endings is the thorny part of writing—the part where what you've lived through and seen with your own eyes drops off and you're left with all the work. That's the moment when you harness up your imagination, like a mule to a plow, and whip it until it moves.

BY ITSELF, THEN, WHAT happened that day on our once-verdant ranch was neither dramatically significant nor especially unique. It took a perceptive creative writing teacher to make me probe deeper—to define the fire in terms of PEOPLE. He made me recall that my mother left the ranch long after I did, unwilling to abandon her home until the last minute, then forced to rocket down the dirt road between towering, flaming trees. He made me think about what became of her afterwards. (That part, I had to make up.) Unless I saw the tempering of her character—of all our characters—in a molten setting, the fire was just a fire. Had I really been a coward? Did the fire pit my timorousness against Jimmy Deetz's natural guts? Did I ultimately become braver?

FOR UNKNOWN REASONS, IT took me forever to understand that the important aspect of dramatic moments seldom lies in the moment itself, but in what I, as a writer, make of it.

Suffice it to say that the lesson kept coming unstuck, and I had to keep gluing it back on as I struggled to turn real life events into gripping stories.

In my lifetime I have lived through, besides the fire, a near-drowning in an undertow, the raising of six boisterous children, the unthinkable loss of two sons, a cataclysmic upheaval in my marriage, the death of a beloved son-in-law, and the shredding of my youngest son's life by addiction. Heaven knows I never sought or expected any of these things (except for the kids, of course).

So why did they all happen?

Nobody can say. But occasionally I have a phantom conversation with a Being I can't identify, and that Being says, "So, Maralys, you always wanted to be a writer . . . you've carried an inner vision, you dreamed of finding drama in real life and sharing it with the world.

Right? . . . Okay, then, I'll just give you something to write about!"

ALLAN CAME BACK FROM camp to find our forest gone.

Nobody died; nobody was even injured. Strangely, the Deetzes, who had less to lose than we did, lost almost nothing that mattered to them. They still had their meadows, their cows, their house, a barn.

For the rest of us—my mother, Hans, Allan, and me—the change in our lives was irrevocable. With the forest consumed, the guest ranch my mom and Hans were putting together became nothing but a vanished dream. The new house they'd been building, unfinished but already occupied by Allan and me, was gone, marked only by two tall chimneys.

For months the atmosphere was bleak. The very air around us stank of charred wood and ashes. At first I felt suffocated, unable to breathe. But my mother and Hans chose to stay on, for reasons I can't now define.

Every day that fall Allan and I packed our lunches and trudged down the dirt road to meet the school bus. We walked between ghostly trees that were still smoldering, and tree stumps that still flamed and sizzled around the roots. Though he'd never done this before, Allan often stopped to relieve himself into some flaming stump or other, intent on drowning the enemy. It was his way of fighting back. A male thing.

I watched his back and waited, and we went on. His nine-year-old efforts didn't strike me as doing much for the situation. But at least they were diverting.

WE LIVED AMONG OUR blackened trees for a couple more years, until World War II came and Mom's marriage fell apart.

With the once-lush trees mere skeletons, there was less to see or care about outside the house, and I found myself reading more than ever. Mom subscribed to the *Reader's Digest*, a lucky circumstance for me, because she was far too distracted and upset to be much of a mother and, without knowing it, she gave the raising of her daughter to a magazine.

*Reader's Digest* isn't paying me to say this, though they should, but it's amazing how much influence a magazine with an attitude can have on an impressionable pre-teen. Among those pages I found a strong voice commanding me to morality and ethics.

Even more, I became steeped in a can-do, Horatio Alger, success-against-the-odds outlook, demonstrated in story after story. After awhile I became convinced I could be stranded in a downed plane on top of a mountain in a raging blizzard and still find a way to extricate myself.

The magazine was amazing. Luckily, on the few occasions my mother paused long enough to share her personal convictions, she was more or less of the same bent as the *Digest*, so together they convinced me that no goal was beyond reach.

Not a bad attitude if you hope to succeed in the Arts.

As I LEARNED OVER the years and proclaimed so vehemently in the first chapter, attitude is essential to writing success. Attitude keeps you striving, attitude makes you search more than once for that exact right word, attitude makes you a life-long student—always analyzing, constantly studying the craft.

Eventually the good writer sees that there are subliminal "rules" for good writing, small, barely-visible techniques that go unnoticed by those merely reading for pleasure.

In the next chapter, I describe a few of the techniques that kept hitting me as I corrected student manuscripts . . . and more, those that occurred to me as I mushed on to become a better writer myself.

Chapter Four

# TECHNIQUES OF THE WRITING CRAFT

To PROVE THAT SOME of us, at least, will always need a critique group, that you can have keen insights into our craft without being flawless, I'm willing to report what some of my fellow critiquers said about the first submitted version of this chapter: "You start out pretty stuffy, like a thirties school marm. Nobody wants to see the chalk scraping across the blackboard."

Another added, "We could see you standing stiffly in the American Gothic—next to the farmer with the pitchfork." That bad, huh?

My group had created an indelible image—the prim schoolteacher with a pencil in her bun. Not me at all. As the author, I hadn't noticed any of this, the stuffiness or the rigidity. "Thanks," I said, and was thinking, as I'd done so often: This is what I pay you for.

Here, then, is a second attempt.

As ALL WRITERS LEARN over time, there are tricks to creating decent sentences. Tricks for expressing ideas clearly. And subliminal techniques for making one's work shine—a mysterious process that can metamorphose into sorcery. Great writing is elusive. I read my favorites over and over: Harper Lee; Bill Bryson; Ivan Doig; Ann Patchett. I see the result, but am never quite sure how they got there.

It's the move from adequate to brilliant that consumes so much time and requires so much practice—that drives authors to write and rewrite and rewrite again. But have hope: writing well does get easier, and eventually the really subtle techniques seep into your subconscious ... until one day you realize you've written some mighty sweet stuff without half trying.

A couple of techniques occurred to me as I struggled with my own writing. In fact, I honestly thought I'd invented them from scratch until a wise student brought me a sixty-year-old grammar book and I saw them dismayingly on the printed page. It was like imagining you'd invented the automobile, only to find one chugging toward you over a stubbly field.

But never mind, the truly indelible rules are those you glean from crossing out and starting over.

The more you work at writing, the more you'll notice that whatever you're trying to say, you can always find a better way to say it.

In case anyone thinks that "voice"—the style or technique of a given author—is unimportant and content is everything, think of James Herriot, whose small stories about the daily life of an English veterinarian are, in themselves, not of great moment. He is, after all, writing about relatively unimportant matters ... about the ailing cow, dog, or sheep on a Yorkshire farm, and about the farmers who fret over their animals. It's all simple, low-key material, nothing intrinsically dramatic. His books contain no murders, sex, romance, intrigue, or violence. The stakes are minimal, certainly not important beyond the boundaries of a given country farm.

Then why do we care?

We care because of James Herriot's own view of the veterinarian's life, because of his keen eye for understated drama, and even more because of his way with words, his utterly charming use of the English language. In Herriot's hands, small incidents loom large, tiny matters swell with importance. His word choices and sentence arrangements are so delightful and his images so precise that we revel in everything he has to say.

Here's an example, from *Memories of a Wartime Vet*: "They say an eavesdropper never hears anything good about himself, and I knew the sensible thing would be to get out of there immediately rather than hear this man vilifying me in a crowded bar. But of course I didn't get out. I stayed, morbidly fascinated, listening with every nerve and fiber."

Ample proof that voice is everything struck me the day I discovered one of Herriot's quaint episodes paraphrased in *Parade Magazine*. The story was about fooling a baby sheep into nursing with the hide of its mother placed over another ewe. In the hands of a different writer making different word choices, the story was nothing. Utterly flat, wholly uninteresting. Only because I knew the original version intimately, did I realize it wasn't the incident itself that contained the charm, but rather Herriot's piquant take on it.

WHILE IT MIGHT SEEM fifth-grade-ish to discuss the fine points of crafting sentences, I've discovered through years of teaching that you can't present lofty ideas without sharp, distinctive sentences. When I'm reading a student's work (and I read about a hundred student pages a week), the sentences are all I've got to go on.

I always feel terrible that I can't focus instead on the forest, but I'm forced to look at the work tree by tree, because that's what is on the page. If the trees are bereft of leaves or covered in blight, there's hardly any forest to observe.

Here, then, is what I've picked up about technique:

1. *When arranging sentences, save the best for last.*

Pull out the strongest, most vivid words and deliver them at the end. The last word—or words—in a sentence tend to ring in a reader's head, and you want those to be the words with the most power . . . the strongest images . . . the greatest emotional impact. Your goal is to leave sentence after sentence reverberating in your reader's mind, until he thinks of you as a dynamite writer.

Example: "Death is what I've always feared," has far less impact than: "What I've always feared most is death." In fact, if the word "death" appears anywhere in a sentence, it should be the final word.

Example: "A shot rang out from the back of the room," focuses on the room and carries less weight than: "From the back of the room came a shot."

Example: "I fell into the river one day at noon when I was hot," conveys a smaller message than: "It was noon, and I was hot, and somehow I fell into the river."

Example: "Like the blast from a hand grenade, the news came at me with stunning force." Better: "The news came at me with stunning force, like the blast from a hand grenade."

As powerful sentences pile up, one after the other, the reader retains an impression that the piece is memorable, and yes, important. Some writers have an innate sense about constructing sentences for maximum impact, the way some actors know instinctively which words to emphasize. But for those who don't, it's a trick that's easily learned.

2. *Put the "set-up" part of a sentence first, and the action last.*

Example: "She found the diamond at the end of the day, after hours of searching." This sentence evokes only a faint image . . . far less than: "At the end of the day, after hours of searching, she found the diamond."

Example: "They clambered to the top of the hill before lunch." What's important here, anyway—the lunch or the climb? Obviously, it's better said, "Before lunch, they clambered to the top of the hill."

Of all the changes I make in student manuscripts, phrase-switching ranks among the top four or five tasks—moving the set-up part to the beginning and the action, or "what happens" to the end. A small matter, yes, but one of those little tricks that, with repetition, creates more powerful writing.

3. *Vary the lengths of sentences.*

Most of my students know this, yet seldom realize they're writing one medium-length sentence after another—unaware that they've gotten into a monotonous, droning pattern that lacks drama or rhythm. It's easy enough to spot a string of too-short sentences; they jump out at you with an "I am Mary. You are Bob." quality. It's harder to diagnose the mid-length sentence disease.

Most top-notch writers are willing, occasionally, to write a sentence that goes on and on, with clause after clause, forming a string of words that don't allow you to take a breath or even pause, yet somehow convey meaning exceptionally well and with plenty of drama. The same goes for short sentences. Even two-word sentences.

Example: (From *One Summer in Between*, by Melissa Mather—one of my all-time favorite books.) "Tonight we had a cookout, just for larks. I mean, there wasn't any need to, the kitchen was still there in the old house . . . . What could I do but act as if I thought the whole idea was absolutely splendid, and help lug the contents of the kitchen and the dishes and the silverware and salt and pepper and pickles and catsup and the coffee and the salad and the rolls and the hot dogs down the lane and through the stone wall and up to the field to where the fireplace was, and I didn't think I ought to grumble because for each of my trips, the children took three."

There's a *reason* for varying your sentences. Boredom. Don't ask me why, but in the written word, repetition of any kind (unless done on purpose for dramatic effect), is boring.

4. *Vary the structure of sentences.*

This is one of the trickier tricks. Beginning writers tend to write as they speak: Subject, verb, object.

Example: "I walked downtown to see the boats." "She put on her jacket and left."

These simple sentences do convey meaning; their simplicity is no big deal and perfectly all right most of the time. But give the reader a whole page of simple sentences and he begins to notice other things in the room, like dust on the coffee table, and you've lost him.

AS A BEGINNING WRITER, I had the awful impression that my writing had all the fascination of *Fun with Dick and Jane,* and I was horrified at the thought of never rising above such mundane composition. Not knowing what else to do, I jotted down a long list of prepositions and taped it above my typewriter: Before. After. As. From. Beside. Since. Under. Over. Above. Beyond. Until. . . . and others. From time to time I simply chose one of those words, arbitrarily, as a way of starting a sentence. "Above my head, the idea floated away from me, a cloud I couldn't quite capture."

Gradually, from those days of being so crassly deliberate, complexity began to sneak up on me like a pervasive cologne until it finally took over my efforts and I am now sometimes cautioned by fellow writers to unwind and simplify.

For those who don't naturally think in sophisticated prose, I maintain elegant variation can be learned. Deliberately. But first you have to believe that not writing elegantly, ever, is a serious problem.

5. *Avoid sentences overburdened with clauses.*

Occasionally I see a student sentence that is so overloaded with clauses it's like a waitress staggering under dishes stacked up both arms. You read it, hearing in your head a metaphorical crash.

Example, from a recent student manuscript: "Arriving at the unused first floor of the studio, I shifted the bags to my left arm so I had a free hand to open the glass door to the stairs leading to the second floor."

This from a good-natured student who is working hard at her craft and could see that the sentence had ballooned out of control. Knowing her, she had it fixed by morning.

6. *Use fewer adjectives and adverbs—and stronger nouns and verbs.*

Example: Instead of "steep mountain," which conveys only limited meaning, use "precipice," "crag," "peak," "pinnacle," "escarpment," "promontory," or "cliff," all of which offer much sharper images.

Example: Instead of "tall, muscular man," try "giant," "gorilla," "behemoth," "muscle-man," "pugilist," "Goliath," "big-foot." The greater number of sharp, evocative nouns you sprinkle into your writing, the fewer adjectives will be necessary. (And here might be the place to say, buy a thesaurus and use it. Mine sits right beside the computer. Each time I look up a word I circle it in red, and there are now circled words on more than half the pages.)

The same principle applies to verbs and their modifiers.

Example: Instead of, "He ran fast," which offers only a generalized image, use, "He raced," "He tore," "He zoomed," "He streaked," "He burst," all strong verbs that don't require an adverb. As Stephen King says, "The adverb is not your friend." King suggests that authors avoid adverbs at all costs, which seems laudable, if somewhat extreme.

Certainly in the romance genre, adverbs were once used so often in lieu of strong verbs, that in the mid-80s they threatened to turn the genre into a joke. Dialogue was all too often followed with silly adverbs like, "she said breathily," "he said cattily," "she replied moodily," "he said harshly," and simple verbs were too often modified in terms like, "He waved stiffly," "She blushed fetchingly."

7. *Be specific, not general.*

Example: "She gazed at the field of flowers," conveys a non-specific image. Turn the field into poppies and suddenly the sentence becomes sharper. Flowers, in fact, should never be just flowers, but always a particular kind—roses, jonquils, tiger lilies, asters. Your choice. Even to the reader who cares not a hoot about flowers and doesn't know one from another, a stronger image is formed when the word is specific.

Instead of dog, use Airedale, Scotty, German Shepherd, poodle, terrier, white Labrador, anything to pin down that familiar creature and take it out of the generic trash can.

8. *Upgrade your dialogue; make your characters sound brilliant.*

Story dialogue should sound better than most people speak . . . brighter, wittier, pithier. You, the lucky writer, have more time than everyday people to think up great comebacks, wonderful little zingers, erudite thoughts, clever witticisms, deep philosophical observations.

Spend your dialogue on all the most sprightly, vital words that you've ever heard people say, and skip the witless stuff that people in grocery stores spout every time you buy a quart of milk. Never, ever, ever, have a character say, "Have a nice day."

Such prosaic greetings as, "Good morning," "How do you do?" "Please come in," "May I take your coat?" "How are you?" "I'm fine," and the ubiquitous, "Have a nice day," should never be part of written dialogue because they all come off as unbearably dull.

Instead of employing quotes for commonplace transitions, use condense-devices like, "They said their good-byes and left." Or, "Introductions over, she said, 'My God, Harry, you've gained forty pounds!'"

When novel characters speak, they skip right to the heart of the matter, to the core of whatever they're trying to convey. Great dialogue from great writers echoes in our heads. "As God is my witness, I'll never be hungry again!"

To the beginning writer who cries out, "But I want my dialogue to be realistic!" the answer is, the written word can never be truly realistic because most of life is boring—and most of what people say is tedious. The writer who wants perfect realism need only follow a few ordinary mortals around with a tape recorder to discover why drama, not realism is the goal.

While we're at it, my guess is that even Winston Churchill and Abraham Lincoln did not speak in ringing rhetoric at home. (Well, maybe Churchill did.) Certainly Lincoln's most memorable words were much-pondered in advance and, some say, revised and polished to bring them to their ultimate luster.

AND NOW SOME ADDITIONAL tiny admonitions:

9. *Make your writing active, not passive.*

Active sentence construction, in which people do things, instead of having things done to them, is infinitely stronger, and nearly always the way to go.

Example: "Her sweater was put on, and her hat adjusted," as though a magic hand appeared from the ether and did these things to her. Weak. Weak. Weak. "She pulled on her sweater and adjusted her hat," puts us right into the action.

10. *Avoid using "was" and "were" as helping verbs.* Pale, limp writing results from these unnecessary, tagged-on additions to ordinary verbs. "She was chasing the bird," lacks the punch of, "She chased the bird." "He was speaking slowly, in a droning voice," is inferior to, "He spoke slowly, in a droning voice." Even better would be, "He droned on."

A quick caution. I've had students/writing purists who've proclaimed (because of some other writing class), that the words "was" and "were" carry a fatal taint and thus should be avoided forever . . . and in the process those students went to extraordinary lengths to circumvent the past tense forms of the perfectly good verb "To Be."

Nonsense. The words "was" and "were" have legitimate uses, and any attempt to eschew them completely becomes obsessive and clumsy . . . or just plain silly.

A final word about style. As a teacher, I'm nothing if not pragmatic. If it works, it works. There are times when all the above "rules," can and should be broken. Times when, for effect, the best, most memorable construction in the world is to fly in the face of a given adage and do it your own way.

I love variety and applaud originality and a bold lack of convention. Sometimes my students raise their hands and protest, "But Maralys, you said . . ." and they're throwing back at me one of my own cautions, and that's when I'm forced to say, "That's true, but in this case it works."

In the long run, if it works and we love the way it reads, that's all that matters.

Chapter Five

# A Seed Takes Root

I'll never know why my mother did most of the things she did . . . why she suddenly decided to leave the ranch in the middle of the night, gathering up Allan and me and our new baby brother like so many duffle bags and once more dragging us all away. Perhaps it had something to do with a growing rift between her and Hans.

At any rate, Allan and I abruptly found ourselves living in a boarding house in Berkeley—with a mother and a two-year-old, but no stepfather and no explanations.

"Where's Hans?" we asked.

"He's not here," Mom said testily. "Your new school is just down the street. You can walk."

We did, and everything was different. No sense anymore that Allan and I owned the road and all that lay around it; no dramatic snowstorms whistling down from Mt. Eddy to buffet our faces and blanket the dirt road; no more trudging a mile through drifts, with all those feelings of *Gee, we made it!* as we boarded the school bus with our boots full of snow.

But we did have electricity.

The war started for the U.S. in December, another unexpected upheaval that blended strangely with our personal family chaos. I remember Hans stopping by to take me and Allan Christmas shopping for our mother. He was so pathetic my heart melted for him; I sensed he was near tears. We went from store to store as though no amount of effort would be too much. "Do you think your mother will like this?" holding up a pink negligee. "Should I buy this bracelet?" "How about perfume?" dabbing a bit on the back of his hand. "What do you think, kids—what would she want?" His voice was nothing like I'd ever heard it—sad and sometimes quavering. "I love your mother so much." The yearning, the pain were enough to draw us right into his camp.

Allan and I desperately wanted to help him, but we didn't know **what** our mom wanted. We came away ready to storm our mother's steely heart and tell her how rotten she'd been to Hans.

"I'm going to talk to Mom," Allan said, because he was just naturally the kindest member of the family.

"Me too. Why is she so mean?" So there we were, Allan and I, unwittingly steeped like tea bags in the hot emotional waters of adult love. Without many words from either Hans or Mom, we still soaked up all their troubled feelings. The uncertainty. The anger. The pain.

Looking back, I think what my mom wanted most was for Hans to stop having affairs.

OUR STINT AT BERKELEY lasted only six months. The next few years were like a trip through a clothes dryer, with parts of the family spinning off in different directions. Mom sent me to Rochester, New York, to spend an exhilarating year with her sister, who lavished time on me like jewels. I said ordinary things and my aunt and her live-in maid listened and smiled and nodded, and when I became truly inspired and stretched my stories into the absurd, reaching for humor, they *laughed*. No one had ever done that before. *Please,* I'd be thinking, *let's not stop. Let's nobody go to bed.*

The rest of the family traveled to strange cities in states I never visited, following our newly-enlisted Hans wherever he was stationed. The adults had decided to give their marriage another chance. When my mother finally floated back to earth long enough to buy a house, she landed in Denver, because Hans, with his Swiss background, was assigned to the Rockies as an army ski instructor.

At the end of summer she phoned. "You can come home now, honey," she said, and my aunt reluctantly put me on a train to Denver. "I'll miss you, Sweety. I do hate to see you go back to being the tail on your mother's kite."

Though Hans drifted in and out of our lives during the Denver years, his presence no longer seemed to matter much, at least not to me. I was off to East High, then The University of Denver.

As a freshman at the university, I fancied myself as a nifty writer, though with what credentials remains a mystery; I can't honestly remember writing anything. Still, an English professor said to me unexpectedly, "You do have a way with words," which suggests she must have seen some bit of work that I no longer recall.

THE UNIVERSITY OF DENVER was a streetcar school. Always the elitist, Mother made me believe I could do better. "Honey, why don't you apply to Colorado U? Or even Stanford?" If she could sail her tall ship into Smith College, her daughter should certainly be able to navigate a dinghy into Stanford.

Stanford? Mom didn't know what she was talking about. She was sadly uninformed. The school was famous then for its reluctance to admit females, for maintaining a deliberate ratio of three men to one woman. Its snootiness was legendary and off-putting; if you were a woman, you might as well forget it.

Before I quite dismissed the idea, however, my *Reader's Digest* mother threw in a few words about quitting before I ever tried . . . about overcoming flood, fire, famine, futility, and the Stanford Aptitude Test.

Suddenly determined, I found a tutor and spent the summer learning vocabulary words: memorized them, used them in sentences, repeated them back to myself, discussed their subtleties with the tutor, tried to make them part of my everyday language.

Thanks to our German father, Allan and I have been known to exhibit all the obsession of the entire Teutonic race. When we do something, we **really do it**. But luck played a role in bringing me a mentor who knew precisely which, out of our limitless supply of

English words, ought to be memorized and, as it turned out, which might prove useful for a writer.

My first look at the English portion of the test itself was nothing short of thrilling. As I sat there sizing up questions, I realized with a start that there wasn't a word on the page I didn't know. When the test asked, "This is to this as that is to X," it helped to know what the "This" and the "That" meant. Never had test-taking been so satisfying . . . until I hit the math.

Even a tutor hadn't been able to drag me out of the wasteland I'd created with years of inattention to figures. After a few inept stabs at computations, I answered the math questions by muttering under my breath, Well, I haven't had a "C" answer in awhile, guess I'll pick "C."

When I discovered later that I'd been placed in Group One among new sophomore admittees, it seemed Stanford must have marked its girls *up* for demonstrating skills in English and *down* for superiority in math, because there certainly weren't any math skills cluttering up my record.

JUST AS I DECIDED it was time—finally—to take a serious creative writing class, I met my future husband.

I was eighteen, it was the start of summer quarter at Stanford, and Rob Wills and I had just met at a school dance quaintly labeled a "Jollyup," but which the senior girls sneeringly referred to as The Meat Market.

Rob was unlike anyone I'd ever met. He was too short, only six feet tall, and he asked too many blunt questions. For our first date, he invited me to a beach party, which I assumed meant "fraternity." I said yes, imagining I might meet someone taller who wasn't so embarrassingly bent on probing into my life.

I could not have been more surprised to find our "party" consisted of a male acquaintance named Hudson Bowlby—Rob hardly knew him—waiting outside my dorm with his model-T, ready to drive us to the beach.

"This is a *beach party*?" I said in dismay as we squeezed into Bowlby's jalopy, and Rob grinned and said, "Sure it is. I've brought grape juice and peanuts and cheesy crackers. And we're going to the beach."

Only later did he admit, "Bowlby had the only car I could lay my hands on."

The summer was like that—Rob producing one surprise after another. Neither a nerd nor a party boy, he fit no discernable category, so I never knew what to expect. He never did the usual thing—never summoned me with the buzzer in the lobby, but instead stood under my window and whistled. Newly showered, with water still dripping off his brown hair, he blew a three-note tune, blissfully unmindful that all the girls on my side of the building knew he was there, whistling for his puppy to come out and play.

Still, unlike most men, he was a talker; I found him fascinating.

Academically, we ruined each other's summers. Rob was nearly buried by courses in Organic Chemistry and Qualitative Analysis, a year's worth of work condensed into one summer.

I was enrolled in Creative Writing, expected to break out with a major, publishable work.

Instead we went to the library and passed notes back and forth, or we spread a blanket under a shade tree and ostensibly sat there working.

Little of what we did qualified as studying.

Finally, desperate to write **something**, I hastily typed a slice-of-life piece about poor people in a bar ... all intensity and sadness and dark feelings.

I thought my piece was wonderful; and never mind that I'd never been to a bar and didn't know any poor people. The rest, the big work, would come later, when I scraped up sufficient time. Meanwhile, the professor would surely see me as a budding Steinbeck. I waited breathlessly for his words of praise.

Not much was written on my returned paper, just a terse, "Not bad for its sort. But its sort has been overdone."

Really. How was I to know? I was only eighteen. The word "hackneyed" was included in his comments. Unfortunately, I knew what it meant. Reading his few words over and over, I felt the air escaping from my balloon. Psssst, psssst, until I was flat and empty.

After that I couldn't think of a thing to put on paper. Not that I tried often or for long at a time, only that desperation loomed ever larger as the summer quarter faded and no ideas presented themselves. I mean none. Zilch. The teacher hadn't liked my intense little piece, wet with tears, and probably didn't care that I'd given it my last two ounces of passion.

Looking back, it was like expecting to get milk from a cow that spends her days dashing up and down the meadow. What did I **think** I would write if I never sat still long enough for a single idea to brew?

About two weeks before quarter's end, when my fellow classmates were handing in their book-length manuscripts, I rushed to my professor with a form that said Incomplete. He scribbled his signature and I promised to return with something . . . sometime. The "what" or the "when" were a bit vague.

Two quarters later, after Rob and I had transferred, briefly, to San Jose State, (Stanford wasn't keen on his grades, either), I marched back to my Creative Writing teacher with a fistful of papers I'd written for a course in Child Psychology. Again, the professor scribbled his signature and gave me a "C" without so much as a glance at my work. The "C" was undeserved, at least for that course. But it wasn't a total cheat. Those same papers had earned me an "A" in Child Psychology.

FAST FORWARD TO MARRIAGE. A tiny tract house. Motherhood.

Now, at last, I was finding things to write about.

The trouble was, I kept having children . . . more and more, until our house reverberated with five boys and a girl. My brain, my inner contemplative self, began filling with stories—if only there was time to get them down.

Books like *Life With Father, Eight is Enough*, and *Please Don't Eat the Daisies*, reinforced my conviction that stories about funny families were selling. It seemed clearer than clear that our own family was as bizarre and nutty as the rest.

By the mid-Sixties I'd started a saga called *Rough Around the Edges*. Since it was impossible to **think** in a house that shudders with activity and echoes with noise, I borrowed the keys to the Little Red

Schoolhouse where the youngest of our children attended pre-school, hired a babysitter, and departed during the dinner hour to write. If a mother intends to escape during any part of the day, there is no better time than dinner—the hellish, five-to-seven hours of cranky children and guaranteed bedlam.

For months I wrote madly, assuming that because I was such a voracious reader, I would just naturally be a publishable writer. Which is not unlike attending a hundred piano concerts and assuming you can play the piano.

Hadn't an English professor told me I had a way with words? Hadn't I always pictured myself as an author?

I wrote the whole book and sent it off to my father for his approval. I assumed he'd love it.

My dad was a doctor whom I'd seen only a few times as I was growing up, thanks to his living in the East while we lived in the West. Still, I knew from his letters and many published articles that he had a way with words, whether I did or not. He was as much a medical politician as a doctor, and his writings had flair and seemed to find their way into dozens of niches, including—I gasped when I saw them—my beloved *Reader's Digest.*

My Dad—we called him "Ted," as did the children in his second family—had expressed a lively interest in Allan and me, especially after we were both grown and married. Ted visited us quite a few times and seemed like the sympathetic sort of man who would adore whatever I wrote and hope to see his oldest daughter as an author.

The last part is true. He *did* want to see me as an author . . . he just didn't think I was one yet. "Perhaps you should study some humorous books," he said, "with stories similar to those you're trying to write. I recommend Betty MacDonald's *Onions in the Stew.*"

I read the book . . . no more, I **studied** the book . . . and the difference between her words and mine was suddenly graphic, almost chilling.

She was a writer and so far I wasn't.

AMONG THE THOUSAND THINGS I needed to learn was how to start a book, a skill I acquired only after many painful attempts.

But it's such a crucial early lesson that the next chapter is devoted entirely to Beginnings.

Chapter Six

# BEGINNINGS

THERE IS NO HARDER job than penning the opening lines of a book. Whatever the genre, it's as though you've been granted one minute to sell an editor on your 400-page manuscript. With each discarded attempt, you recognize anew the difficulty of capturing the soul of a piece in only a few lines. Or if not the soul, at least a tantalizing moment, an outrageous attitude, a startling event, or a compelling story question.

Worse, the requirement intensifies if the book is a novel or memoir . . . meaning if the opening's no good, you might as well toss out the rest of the book.

Opening lines are so demanding that I've learned to loathe, fear, deplore, and agonize over them. Are these few sentences good enough, can they be made still better, shall I ruthlessly delete them and start over?

I'm not alone; all striving authors, those who haven't made it big, quake before the Almighty Opening Lines. (It's interesting to note that the requirement diminishes as literary fame increases—meaning you'll see some pretty saggy beginnings from best-selling authors.)

The importance of openings is expounded endlessly by speakers at writers' conferences, who impart as a dark secret what few editors or agents will admit publicly: if you don't hook them in the first few lines, the rest of your book doesn't matter. It's history. And indeed, I once spent an afternoon helping an agent friend cull through her pile of manuscripts, and there I was, dishing out quick rejections just like all those meanies that so terrorize aspiring writers. The rumors were true; a dull beginning simply doesn't bode well for the rest of the book.

One conference lecturer told us about a colleague who spends endless hours crafting the opening lines of her books, which he considers among the best in the business. Then he added with a smile, "Her beginning lines are always so polished, so nearly perfect, the rest of her book has no hope of living up to them."

I remember groaning inwardly: *Oh, Lord, you mean the whole book has to be perfect?*

WHAT CONSTITUTES A GOOD beginning, anyway?

The quick, useless answer is, anything that makes you eager to read on . . . that raises irresistible story questions.

Specifically, good beginnings employ all sorts of tactics. One of the best is *Attitude—an Opinion/Mind-set/Emotional Bias* for or against something.

Example: (*The Catcher in the Rye* by J.D. Salinger): "If you really want to hear about it, the first thing you'll probably want to know is where I was born, and what my lousy childhood was like, and how my parents were occupied and all before they had me, and all that David Copperfield kind of crap, but I don't feel like going into it."

Example: (*Keys to Rebecca* by Ken Follett): "The last camel collapsed at noon. It was the five-year-old white bull he had bought in Gialo, the youngest and strongest of the three beasts, and the least ill-tempered: he liked the animal as much as a man could like a camel, which is to say that he hated it only a little."

The *Element of Surprise* works well:

Example: (Romance novel, author unknown): "From the waist down, he looked promising."

Example: (*Windmills of the Gods* by Sidney Sheldon): "Stanton Rogers was destined to be President of the United States. He was a charismatic politician, highly visible to an approving public, and backed by powerful friends. Unfortunately for Rogers, his libido got in the way of his career. Or, as the Washington mavens put it: 'Old Stanton fucked himself out of the presidency.' "

Example: (*Through the Narrow Gate*, by Karen Armstrong): "It was 14 September 1962, the most important day of my life. On the station platform my parents and my sister, Lindsey, were clustered together in a sad little knot, taking their last look at me. I was seventeen years old and was leaving them forever to become a nun."

Example: (*Running from the Law* by Lisa Scottoline): "Any good poker player will tell you the secret to a winning bluff is believing it yourself."

*A Tragedy of Some Kind (or a Hint of Tragedy)*, especially a Death, can be a compelling hook. And here I shamelessly offer my own memoir.

Example: (*Higher than Eagles*, by Maralys Wills): "I never thought we'd lose a son to hang gliding. It just never seemed possible that the sport we'd watched and applauded—the sport we'd taken on as a business and nurtured from infancy—could turn around and bite us. And Eric! How could it have been our third son, Eric, they called about, when all along it was Bobby who took the risks, Bobby who'd made a private pact with Luck?"

Example: (*The Lovely Bones* by Alice Sebold) "My name was Salmon, like the fish; first name, Susie. I was fourteen when I was murdered on December 6, 1973."

Example: (*Eric*, by Doris Lund) "Good friends have said, 'But how did it begin? You must have seen it coming.' No one could have seen it coming. This had been a summer like many others . . . "

Example: (*The Joy Luck Club* by Amy Tan) "My father has asked me to be the fourth corner at the Joy Luck Club. I am to replace my mother, whose seat at the mah jong table has been empty since she died two months ago. My father thinks she was killed by her own thoughts. 'She had a new idea inside her head,' said my father. 'But before it could come out of her mouth the thought grew too big and burst. It must have been a very bad idea.' "

*Strong Mood/Atmosphere* can provide a compelling start.

Example: (*The Old Man and the Sea* by Ernest Hemingway): "He was an old man who fished alone in a skiff in the Gulf Stream and he had gone eighty-four days now without taking a fish."

Example: (*Scatterpath* by Maralys Wills): "James Higgins was suddenly fed up with disasters. Eleven consecutive months of viewing charred bodies and reconstructing the mangled chunks of jet engines had left him drained and ready to hang up his job."

Example: (*The Summer of the Barshinskeys* by Diane Pearson): "The first time I saw Mr. Barshinskey he was strolling across Tyler's meadow with a fiddle under his arm. He was singing at the top of his voice in a language none of us could understand, and around the crown of his black hat was a garland of buttercups."

Example: (*Angela's Ashes* by Frank McCourt): "My father and mother should have stayed in New York where they met and married and where I was born. Instead, they returned to Ireland when I was four, my brother, Malachy, three, the twins, Oliver and Eugene, barely one, and my sister, Margaret, dead and gone. When I look back on my childhood I wonder how I survived at all. It was, of course, a miserable childhood: the happy childhood is hardly worth your while. Worse than the ordinary miserable childhood is the miserable Irish childhood, and worse yet is the miserable Irish Catholic childhood."

***Thoughtful, Interesting Observation*** makes for an intriguing start.

Example: (*Onions in the Stew* by Betty MacDonald): "For twelve years we MacDonalds have been living on an island in Puget Sound. There is no getting away from it, life on an island is different from life in the St. Francis hotel. . . . "

Example: (*The Firm* by John Grisham): "The senior partner studied the resume for the hundredth time and again found nothing he disliked about Mitchell Y. McDeere, at least not on paper. He had the brains, the ambition, the good looks. And he was hungry; with his background, he had to be."

A final opening ploy is the use of ***Irony or Humor***.

Example: (*Horowitz and Mrs. Washington* by Henry Denker) "'Mister, a man your age does not resist muggers! You could have got yourself killed!' the irritated cop rebuked Samuel Horowitz in a quite forceful tone. Horowitz sat silent while the nervous young black intern attempted to suture the ugly wound. But he could not keep from thinking, Some doctor! Where did anyone ever get the idea that a black kid could be a good doctor? To be a good doctor, a man had to be Jewish."

Example: (*Why I'm Like This* by Cynthia Kaplan) "There was always one girl at camp whom everyone hated. It had nothing to do with cliques or teams or personal dislikes, and it was not even that everyone had discussed it and a consensus had been raised upon certain irrefutable evidence. It was just like everyone hated lima beans and the color brown. It was obvious and it was universal, so it didn't require organization."

OKAY, THESE AREN'T ALL famous writers.

But it doesn't matter, famous or not, because each of these books has a beginning that is different in some way from the ordinary conversation you'd hear on the street . . different from a newspaper story or most of the written material that comes into your house . . . different from the beginnings of movies, which don't depend on words as a hook. Each poses questions that are so compelling they grab the reader's hand and drag him into the story . . . and though many have properties in common, or rely on more than one tactic, no two are even remotely alike.

After many re-reads of these various beginnings, it strikes me that another element all have in common (besides story questions) is immediacy, an ability to drop the reader quickly into the world of the story. In every one of these beginnings, the book lover is either intrigued with the author's thought processes and opinions, or he is engaged by some dramatic event. The story seems to be already in progress when the reader gets there. Fists are flying, curses fill the air, and the reader just makes it to the balcony, he's just started to peer down.

Furthermore, the story has arrived, or is about to arrive, at some dramatic moment—the beginning of great change, a turning point, a dramatic highlight that will alter the characters forever. It's as though we've happened in at a critical time and are witnessing a vital event—and nothing will ever be the same again. ("I just killed the sonofabitch. So what are you going to do about it?")

When one of my students asks, "Where shall I begin my book?" I always ask in return, "What is the most dramatic thing that happens in your story?" and he tells me.

I say, "Start there."

"But that comes toward the end," he protests.

"That's okay. Start at that moment and work backward."

"But how?"

"Just start there. You'll see, that's the best place. The rest you can figure out."

NOT ONE OF THE above books begins with "background information," and none begin at the "real start" of the events that make up the story. . . .

Think of a book's beginning as a stream rushing down a canyon, and the reader as dropped into the water just as it becomes a waterfall; from that moment on he is carried swiftly downward between looming stone faces, riding high atop the cascading bubbles.

Using the stream analogy, the "back story," or prior events that took place at an earlier time, do not appear at first; they emerge later, as needed, and always a few at a time. Think of the back story as comprised of small tributaries that feed into the larger stream to augment the story when appropriate. But the stream never stops to accommodate past happenings, it just keeps flowing, faster and faster, sweeping today's and yesterday's big moments along with it.

IN MY CLASS WE discuss beginnings a lot. Sometimes, when defending a slow start, a student will protest, "But the reader has to know all these details, he has to know the facts before he'll understand what's going on."

"Not true," I say. "The reader doesn't need to be told most of these things at all. Just relax. Drop your reader into the middle of your story and tell him only as much as he absolutely must know at that moment."

Certain facts, I admit, must be offered early: Where the story is taking place . . . what century it's in . . . the sex and approximate age of the main characters.

Beyond these few essentials, I warn my students not to panic about details. Whatever else the reader needs to know, he'll find out as he goes. And whatever facts are not vitally important, he may never learn at all.

A few of the crucial elements can be supplied as part of the opening lines, and if they're crafted subtly the reader is scarcely aware he's being fed information.

A quick re-read of the eighteen openings above reveals the gender and approximate age of the protagonist in at least fifteen of the eighteen—information given so casually that the reader assimilates it without much thought.

Sometimes "place" is immediately important and sometimes it's not. Nevertheless, most of the above stories manage to convey location within a mere few lines: A desert near the town of Gialo; Washington D.C.; a train station; a hospital; an island in Puget Sound; a summer camp; Ireland; an Asian gaming table; the Gulf Stream; a meadow.

Unless the opening scene mentions artifacts from a different era—like a buggy whip or stage coach—the reader can assume it's a modern story.

Almost every story is dramatic or hints at drama: A boy hates his parents; the last essential camel dies; a man loses his chance at the presidency; a girl leaves home to become a nun; a son dies; a girl is murdered; a Chinese mother dies. High drama everywhere.

DURING ONE OF MY class discussions on beginnings I said, "Attitude is one of the best ways to start a book. And it can provide story questions as well. You, the writer, can put forth an opinion, a feeling, or a strong mood." On the spot, I made up a couple of attitude beginnings, just to give them the idea. Try this, I said: "I've hated men all my life, so it's a wonder I ever married one. And now that I'm about to get even with this man I've tormented and who's tormented me all these years. . . . "

I tried another. "Marcy had once loved trains. Loved the diesel smell of them, the clackety clack of wheels across uneven tracks. But now she'd been on the train so long that the smell of diesel was masked by the sour odor of unwashed bodies, and the sound, once soothing, seemed a dreaded measure of days passing . . . of a rush to some kind of unwanted fate."

I pointed out that the story questions are right there. In the first example, the reader wonders how the protagonist has been tormented, and why, and how she plans to get even.

In the second, the reader wonders where Marcy is going and why she's been on a train so long, and what will become of her next.

THERE MUST BE A legion of good books I've skipped over because the beginnings were so tedious they felt impenetrable.

On the other hand, maybe there aren't. If the writers weren't craftsmen enough to excite me at the beginning, were they skilled enough to hold my attention later on?

There, I've said it. I've joined all those harsh, judgmental types on the publishing side, and all you aspiring writers who think stodgy beginnings should be overlooked and forgiven are now free to hate me.

## Chapter Seven

# A WRITER THAT NOBODY PAYS

FOR THE SECOND TIME I'd hit the mat, felled first by a Stanford professor and his blunt "hackneyed," and now by my own father.

It occurred to me that many would-be scribes would decide their writing problems were terminal . . . well, hey, I was never meant to be an author anyway.

*But that's not me,* I thought. *This is temporary. I can rise above any disappointment.*

I never would have guessed that my years of rejection were just beginning.

At least my dad was tactful, gracious enough to say that *Rough Around the Edges* did have some funny lines, though it required work. It didn't read like a novel, he said. It lacked distinctive scenes, it needed a sense of going someplace. It was short on description. It was also full of "talking heads," a term my dad didn't know and I only learned about later.

Guessing correctly that I wouldn't have a clue as to what he meant, he give me that suggestion for Betty MacDonald's *Onions in the Stew,* adding, "She's the author of *The Egg and I,* and she does very well what you're trying to do. You'll gain insight by studying how she does it."

Quite by coincidence, I happened to have Betty MacDonald's book in a volume of *Reader's Digest Condensed Books*. With my father's advice ringing in my head, I sat down and began reading.

At first, trying to figure out how the woman did what she did was nearly impossible. The story was so funny, the descriptions so full of unusual imagery, her attitudes so pithy and ironic, that I was swept into her vision—but gleaned few clues about her technique. (I also unwittingly absorbed the shortened, condensed-novel format, which I would later have to un-absorb.)

Three or four more readings made her technique clearer. By then I'd nearly memorized Betty MacDonald's best lines. Writing about Vashon Island in the state of Washington, she called Mount Rainier "that magnificent, unbelievably shy peak who parts her clouds and shows her exquisite face only after she has made sure Uncle Jim and Aunt Helen are really on their way back to Minneapolis."

And later, "Everything on Vashon Island grows with insane vigor and you have the distinct feeling, as you leave the dock and start up the main highway, that you should have brought along a machete."

One of her best scenes had to do with a washing machine brought over from the mainland in a rowboat. The machine was such a beast of a thing, so difficult to control, that the family left it in the boat overnight, tied to the dock.

MacDonald writes, "Sunday morning I got up later, tireder and nastier than I had planned, to find that the washing machine had gotten away after all. Joan and Don with their irritating early-morning cheerfulness and 20/20 vision had spotted it riding the waves like a stout gray lady on an excursion boat."

When the family took another rowboat out to rescue their recalcitrant appliance, " . . . it had slid up and wedged itself in the prow of the rowboat, from which position it stolidly watched our maneuvers to ease alongside and get the painter." And later, "We reached shore at last, the washing machine defiant and uncooperative all the way, and when we tried to maneuver it up the narrow trail to the house it weighed just as much as possible and kept flinging its wringer around its head like a Billy club."

And on and on. I read her book so many times the cover fell off the volume and the pages turned yellow and in places became stained with droplets of tea. Certain passages are underlined worshipfully in pencil. But more important, Betty MacDonald's attitudes and style seeped into my subconscious and began filling the empty spaces. The next time I wrote, I felt like Betty MacDonald. When inspiration turned its back and deserted me, I snatched up her book and read some more. I didn't want to **be** her. I just wanted to be **like** her.

After numerous re-writes and re-namings of my funny book, I sent it off again, once more to my father, but also to two publishers—first one, then another. (In those days perfect photocopies didn't exist. You laboriously typed each page with one or two carbons, but publishers would only consider the original. Simultaneous submissions were simply impossible; nobody had the time or stamina to type a long manuscript twice.)

This time my dad liked it. He must have liked it quite a lot, because he gave it to his wife, his daughters, and his secretary, who claimed she enjoyed it so much she couldn't wait to pick it up again each night.

The publishers were . . . well, publishers. They seldom go crazy over new writers. Actually, sometimes they do, but the manuscripts they seem to swoon over right from the first page are usually so dense, so snobbishly literary, so slow-moving and—mainly inaccessible—that I, as a reader, can seldom wade through more than a few pages before giving up in dismay.

The writers I admire most were always rejected at first—and sometimes rejected a lot. Betty MacDonald's *The Egg and I* was turned down by several publishers, including one whose first-reading editor loved it, but whose in-house committee made her refuse. The editor taped the MacDonald rejection letter above her desk as a reminder of a sad, lost opportunity. "The committee listens to me now," she says.

With the second publisher, a major house, my funny book came close. I wish I'd realized then, how close. The work received such a good "No" that I should have kept going. "Your book has had many readings," they wrote in the rejection. "Unfortunately, the final vote went against it." Which means, from all the wisdom I've since accumulated about publishing, the manuscript should have been re-worked and fine-tuned and polished with all the precision of a diamond cutter and then sent out over and over until someone grabbed it up.

But none of that seemed obvious to me then. In those days two "No"s slammed the door—at least on that book.

Still, I kept sending out manuscripts. Poetry. Short stories. Articles. Essays. How-to's. For fifteen years, an intermittent stream of carefully-crafted words flowed out of our house, all created in stolen hours and interrupted regularly by children. A well-known New York agent took me on but never sold anything.

Quite by accident, I learned that one magazine, at least, has more than one stock rejection slip. *Redbook* turned me down with a Dear Author letter that said, "You write with a facility that has captured our attention." Oh sure, I thought, it's a form letter—you say that to all your rejectees. Not so. Their next rejection was heartless, all cement and no flowers.

AS I LOOKED THROUGH drawers of rejected manuscripts in preparation for writing this book, it became clear that I was a mule whose attention the farmer could never quite get, no matter how hard or how often he clobbered the poor creature over the head. I just wouldn't give up. I saw myself as a writer and, by jinx and by damn and by a sworn oath to the literary gods, I was going to be one.

I saved all my rejections in a shoe box. Each time I dropped another into the box, I pictured myself some day giving speeches and opening the box in front of a vast audience and holding up a fistful. "This is how many rejections you can get before you ever publish anything," I'd say, and tell them the final number. Or maybe I'd tip out the box and pour rejection slips all over the floor. There'd be gasps. Little cries of amazement.

The shoebox filled slowly and from time to time the contents were counted. While I loathed every one, at the same time I also relished them. They were proof that a writer could beat the odds. The more I had, the more triumphant my career would eventually be.

By the end of fifteen years the shoebox was three-quarters full. When, in the future, I gave my exultant, published-author's speech, the audience was going to gasp its head off.

ALL THOSE YEARS WHEN nobody was buying what I wrote, I suppose I was still luckier than some authors, like Stephen King, for instance, who once wondered how he'd buy medicine for his baby.

Though our household had its share of problems, poverty wasn't one of them. "I'm just glad we don't depend on your writing career to eat," Rob said dryly, watching me pack up yet another manuscript. As always, I worked in a frantic hurry, late to pick up a son from a trumpet lesson.

"You wait," I said, "I'll be published someday." (Privately, I was no longer sure.)

"I've **been** waiting, Babe. Forever."

I refused to acknowledge this and sealed the envelope, and as usual he softened. "On the other hand, Vegas odds would definitely go with you and your German resolve. I'd never bet against you." We both knew what he meant. We'd had this talk numerous times, all his observations about my stubbornness and blind persistence and how we Germans never know when we're licked.

"You're in a rotten business, Babe, you know that, it's nothing but a crap shoot. I don't know how you do it—knocking yourself out like this year after year."

"So what's the alternative, Rob? Quit? The Arts have always been terrible, breaking in has always been miserable and deflating. But I don't mind half as much as you do. The writing itself is wonderful, I love every minute spent with words. It's the selling that stinks. You know I'd rather write than do just about anything."

"That's what you say," he said. "So I have to believe you. But from where I sit it's maddening—watching you wrap and stamp and send out. And then watching it all come back. To me, it's insulting. Frankly, it would drive me nuts. I'd never work in an industry where my income depends on someone else's whim."

"It's not about money, Rob. It's never been about money."

Yet it was. In my heart I knew it was; the core issue was money all the way.

In those days I was getting published regularly—at the tennis club, the church, in various in-house magazines—but always for free. No contracts, no checks. They just kept asking for articles and took whatever I wrote. To Rob, to the world—and yes, even to me—I fell short of being an author because I worked for nothing.

"I always read what you write in the club bulletin," a tennis friend said to me one day.

"Oh. Well. Thank you."

"You should try to get published."

I looked at her strangely; what an original idea. "If I do, will you pay to read me?"

The slightest pause. "Why . . . sure."

*That means you won't. But someday you will.*

SUCH AN UNFAIR CONTRAST between Rob and me. He was a lawyer and people paid him do their lawyering and that made him, in everyone's eyes, a professional. I was a writer that nobody paid, which made me a mother with a typewriter.

For all of us who are basically indifferent to money (maybe because we've always had enough), a great truth hangs over our heads, like a tree with a cracked limb. Money is the big separator. Money is where respect lies. Money is what makes you "worth" something.

Even small children know it. When I speak to third and fourth graders (which I do, regularly), the first hand that goes up . . . the first eager, pipey question . . . is always the same: "How much money do you get?"

ANY MOTHER WITH SIX children has a convenient, ready-made excuse for not getting published. Children are inimical to thought, they're hell on concentration. They're worse than an outside job, because they're twenty-four hours on and no hours off. You can't go someplace and forget you know them.

Ironically, though, it was the children who were responsible for my first sale, the kids who ultimately tipped me out of the shoebox.

By then, I knew a little of what appears in the next chapter. I'd begun to recognize some of the small goofs that diminish a manuscript and make it appear less than professional.

Chapter Eight

# SMALL GOOFS

SIX OR SEVEN HOURS a week, I sit on my stationary bike with a red pen and a manuscript, and I pedal and read and stop pedaling and jot down. It's an hour each day I enjoy, because here are all these earnest manuscripts, written by an engineer, a social worker, a roustabout, a football star, a Vietnam vet, an oceanographer, a Dane, a teacher, all different from one another, all full of insights into my students' minds and lives, each rich with details that reveal more about them than they ever dream . . . not to mention some really good stories in which I lose myself week after week.

Yet it's odd that there's a sameness, too, among the small mistakes that lurk in submission after submission, all hiding in different places, most expecting to remain undiscovered. I'm reading merrily along, and then . . . oops! Can't let this little fellow spoil the sentence, must get him out of here. And so comes the crossing out, the re-wording, the transposing, the interlineating.

Each semester, the small goofs gradually fade from the current beginner manuscripts, and by the waning days are mostly eliminated. But then the semester ends, and here comes a new group of writers, and voila! They're making the same errors we've all been fighting so hard to get rid of.

When a manuscript nears perfection, it's still hard to leave alone; a half dozen more sentences will do it, I think, a few extra words here, a fleshing out there. And so even the advanced manuscript comes back to its creator, bleeding red between the lines, just like all the others.

My class is wonderful, if a little different. A dozen students have been with me for years—some for as long as eighteen years. Their manuscripts have become so polished I read them for pleasure, or to find places to add enriching sentences. Few of these writers need real editing. My only regret is that most are so devoted to writing, they aren't equally devoted to getting published.

AMONG THE TINY RULES I keep pulling out of the writing hat are a few cautions I've never read in books; which isn't to say they're not published *somewhere.* . . .

Looking back, I've corrected a lot of work over twenty-one years. According to my dubious math, it adds up to well over five thousand submissions (or fifty thousand pages), enough to provide a fair sampling of the small writing errors that crop up everywhere like pretty little dandelions, each one kind of yellow and innocent, but cumulatively enough to diminish the best-intentioned work.

What follows are trivial observations . . . except for this first one, which is major, but so devious it can sneak into anyone's manuscript (mine too), and make it unintentionally funny.

1. *Misplaced Subjects*

(My term for what is called, technically, a dangling participial phrase). For simplicity it's easier to speak of missing subjects . . . because, as you look at these sentences, by golly you know *something* is missing, and the more you think about it the more you gather that the real subject departed just as the sentence hit the page.

Example, from a recent student manuscript: "Now seated, his feet throbbed from their overactive day."

It isn't the feet that are seated, of course, but the real subject of the sentence—"he"—which has been misplaced and is off in sentence heaven.

Example: "Dashing to my class, three books fell out of my arms and landed in a puddle."

Once again, the books weren't dashing anywhere. The implied "I" is missing and needs to be added.

The misplaced subject problem appears often among our submissions, several times a week, and sometimes I'm startled to find it in something of my own. It's an error that tends to provoke student laughter because we see inanimate objects doing some pretty strange things.

2. *Use of "Proceed to"*

Examples: "He proceeded to set up the chairs." "She proceeded to comb her hair."

This is one of those useless constructions that bog down a sentence while adding nothing to the meaning. I tell my students that nobody should ever "proceed to" do anything—he should just do it.

("Proceed to" reminds me of that empty, spoken phrase, "if you will," that's so dear to the heart of the speaker who can't figure out how to end a sentence.)

3. *Use of diminishing qualifier*

Examples from recent manuscripts: "She bent slightly toward us." "Peter jumped a little." "He laughed somewhat loudly."

In their zeal to be precise, students add qualifying adverbs that do nothing except weaken the image. "He laughed somewhat loudly," lessens the impact of the man's laughter. In almost every case, such qualifiers pull the energy out of the verb, while failing to provide the intended accuracy. If laughter is meant to be weaker than loud, change the verb to something else, like "snickered," or "tittered," or "guffawed."

4. *Use of distracting detail*

Examples: "He raised his left eyebrow." "She carried the glass in her right hand." "They came through the sliding door adjacent to the picture window." "He walked six and three-quarters miles." "An hour and seven minutes later, she left."

It's seldom necessary to distinguish between our left and right body parts . . . or to describe *exactly* where something is located . . . or to pinpoint with perfect accuracy how long something took, or how far away an object is, or what it's made of, or its exact physical dimensions.

I once edited a war novel written by a doctor who thought it necessary to point out the exact size and location and color of every physical object in the story, and to record every distance in specific miles, and to note the technical name, millimeters and descriptive numbers of every plane, gun, and boat . . . until the story began to read like a carefully-drafted munitions contract. Within a page the plot got lost in a maze of detail, and by chapter's end the story line had been shot down by a couple of fifty caliber machine guns at a thousand yards.

In telling us precisely which hand or eyebrow is being used or raised, the writer focuses attention on minutiae and pulls the reader away from the story. When a student writes, "He waved his left hand," I change it to, "He waved," leaving out even the unnecessary mention of a hand. What else do you wave with?

Besides, we don't need to know which hand someone is using. Who cares?

One of our most crotchety, yet most beloved students (now bedridden) railed at his fellow students for years about any character who "shrugged his shoulders," or "nodded his head." Sometimes crude, Ben asked, "What else can you shrug—your ass?" Any student who's still around from those days would never use what we now call a "Benism."

5. *Use of awkward two-word constructions*
Examples: "He was seeming to like it." Or, "She bought outdoor-type carpet." Or, "It was a long, weary-sounding sigh." All three phrases appeared in student manuscripts recently, and in each case the offending word had to be taken out. "Seeming-to" is always awkward. The words "type" and "sounding" when added to adjectives don't do any good, they just sound clumsy.

6. *Use of, "He said as he . . ."*
Though this construction is found over and over in student manuscripts and is not technically wrong, it's neither necessary nor desirable. Characters in a story don't need to be talking over their shoulders as they do something. It's cleaner prose when a character says something, followed by a separate sentence in which he does something—or vice versa—but all in the same paragraph.

Bad Examples: "'You must hate me,' he said as he walked to the bar," has a wordy, unprofessional ring to it. "'I assume this is strictly confidential,' Mitch said as he pulled notes from his pocket."

The second example was stolen (and altered) from John Grisham's *The Firm*. The original is much better. "Mitch pulled the notes from a pocket. 'I assume this is strictly confidential.'" (Note that he didn't say "left pocket.")

Another example of good Grisham writing: "Avery laid the printout on his credenza and frowned at Mitch. 'I just don't want you to burn out or neglect things at home.'"

Almost never does anyone in *The Firm* say something **as** he's doing something else.

This is a small, picky objection, yet it's one of those constructions—a matter of style—that produce weak writing. (I almost said, "weak-sounding" writing, but caught myself.)

Even with this caveat, there are times when it's okay to have the character speak **as** he does something, especially if the two parts are closely related. Example: "'This room is a mess,' he said as he threw clothes in the hamper."

No. No. On second thought, the passage works better without that construction. Example: "'This room is a mess.' He picked up socks, shirts, a pair of pants, and threw them in the hamper."

I'm sticking to my guns.

*7. Use of "There were" or "There was" in descriptions*

Examples: "There were three flower pots along the outside wall." "There was a nude statue in one corner of the room." "There was a cowboy galloping his black horse across the meadow."

Better to offload the "there were" and "there was" in favor of descriptive verbs. Examples: "Three flower pots lined the outside wall." "A nude statue huddled in a corner of the room." "A cowboy galloped his black horse across the meadow."

Sometimes it takes imagination to find the right verb to replace the "there was" construction, but it's always worth the effort and produces stronger, more graphic images.

*8. Use of "if" when you mean "whether"*

All too often, the "if" word is used when "whether or not" is implied....

Example: "She couldn't decide if she should go." Here there's an implied "whether or not," and so the sentence should read, "She couldn't decide whether she should go."

At least half the "ifs" in student sentences need to be replaced by "whether."

9. *Use of synonyms for "said"*

Afraid that they're being repetitious, new authors often rummage madly for synonyms for the common word "said," unaware that it's invisible, and therefore the best choice for dialogue. Most professionals use "said" exclusively, knowing it won't draw attention to itself—that in fact, the dialogue will seem sharper and clearer when the operative tag is the mundane "said."

10. *Repetitious use of "as" in forming sentences*

Too often the word "as" becomes a kind of literary glue, pasting together the two halves of a sentence. When the word "as" is employed more than once within a couple of paragraphs, the construction becomes awkward and noticeable. In most cases, both halves of an "as" sentence are weakened.

Examples from student manuscripts: "The wind drowned out Richard's voice as the sail swayed under the pressure." "He corrected the plane's heading as fighter planes began attacking." "John stumbled across the rocking boat as the captain fought the wheel."

And a final, clause-heavy example: "Henry watched the rudder parting the water in green streaks as the boat surged forward into an increasingly stiffer wind as they left the protection of the cliffs." This one needs a complete overhaul.

The others might be fixed as follows: "Richard shouted at his companion, but the wind drowned out his voice. Ahead of him, the sail swayed under the pressure." "Fighter planes streaked past his cockpit window. Ducking instinctively, he corrected the plane's heading." "Off balance, John stumbled across the rocking boat. Yards away, the captain fought the wheel."

The "as" disease is easily cured, but first it has to be recognized.

Once again, writing cautions come with exceptions. When the two halves of the sentence are closely related, the "as" format works: "His heart swelled with excitement as he felt the boat responding." Here, the two halves actually need each other.

11. *Confusing text*

As authors, we unknowingly create confusion when the scene is in our heads but not on the page. For instance, when several same-sex characters interact in a scene, the reader often can't tell who the "he"—or "she"—refers to. Or, similarly, which object is the antecedent of "it."

Occasionally a character (in a tagless quote), utters words which would suit a couple of different people and I'm forced to scribble, "Who speaks?"

At other times, an author refers casually to an event or minor character that hasn't appeared in the book for chapters, sending the reader on a backwards chase through the pages to refresh his memory.

Technically-oriented writers sometimes refer to equipment or procedures, (or use technical acronyms) about which the average reader has no knowledge.

I've had students argue that this scientific "what's it," or that esoteric behavior was "common knowledge."

Common or not, any time a story becomes confusing and stops someone mid-paragraph, the magic of the piece is lost. It's impossible to remain steeped in a story-line when you've had to re-read a passage several times . . . or look something up . . . or try to fathom what that arcane reference might be.

One day a student smiled and neatly summed things up: *"Confuse 'em and you lose 'em."*

The good news is, most confusing areas are easily fixed.

12. *Unnecessary words*

This is another biggy. Every teacher who expounds on technique says something about trimming excess words. Yet sometimes the unneeded words are so few and so subtle as to be hardly noticeable. Example from a recent student manuscript: "Next time you do this, I'm going to have to whap you upside the head."

The "going to" is unnecessary, easily replaced by "I'll have to . . . " which leaves the meaning intact, while cutting two words. Even simpler would be, " . . . I'm gonna whap you upside the head."

It's an odd truism that the deeper you bury an idea in words, the duller it gets. At the same time, the more ideas you add to a topic, the richer it gets. Which sounds like a contradiction, but isn't.

*A writer's goal is to say more and more while using fewer and fewer words.*

In my novel-writing class trimming a sentence becomes a game, like working a puzzle. How many words can we remove and still leave the meaning intact?

AND NOW A CONTRADICTION: Sometimes eliminating words can ruin a writer's style. Intuitive writers often add words for rhythm, or phrases for effect, and trimming such sentences down to the bones can leave the work as bleached and bare as a carcass picked over by vultures.

So it's a case-by-case call. As in so many artistic endeavors, all editing is judgment—sizing up the material and trimming—or yes, padding—for greatest effect.

Which means the process is like sculpting in clay. As the teacher I'm as apt to add words to an over-lean, skimpy piece as remove them from a submission that's fat and sloppy.

In fact, among all my student manuscripts, thin, minimal writing is a more common error by far than wordy, overblown text, and I'm constantly urging students to enrich their pieces—to build their scenes, add description, include more action, heighten the conflict, and provide the telling details that enhance drama.

Contrary to popular belief, most new writers don't linger long enough as they write their big scenes; they type fast and run for the gate. They say what they have to say and get out, like someone with his pants on fire.

"This has to be fuller," I point out. "The scene should be longer. I need to see the meadow and the corral. I must hear the rusty gate, feel the wind on my arms, smell the manure. Your characters are too mild, they should fly into a rage, their words should cut like knives. This lacks the protagonist's reactions ... what is he thinking, how does he feel?"

In short, what I say most often is, *"Your piece needs drama."*

Of all the problems I encounter in student manuscripts, my fixit list is topped by Skimpy Drama. Without a good supply of rich and dramatic scenes, a novel or memoir has no hope of being published.

And so the next instructional chapter will be devoted to Building Dramatic Scenes.

Chapter Nine

# THANKS TO THE CHILDREN

MY CHILDREN WEREN'T TRYING to get me published. In fact, they no doubt regarded my typewriter as some kind of quaint appendage that seemed welded to my hand when I left the house. Yet when I finally sold something it was because of them . . . because of who they were, and the passions that drove them.

It was Chris, our flying-mad second son, who discovered the exotic world of hang gliding and led all of us down a path that we soon discovered was neon-lit and aglow with excitement.

Together, Chris and his older brother, Bobby, startled the staid beach community of San Clemente by flying down small hills under huge bamboo and plastic kites. I can still see them vividly, their translucent plastic sails crackling in the wind, and the boys, young and laughing, hanging by their armpits from cross-pieces of bamboo . . . dangling above the ground like enthusiastic marionettes, their legs scissoring through space.

From miles around, spectators were drawn to watch, and drivers pulled off the freeway for a better look. Strangers ran up to them exclaiming, "I couldn't believe my eyes. What do you call those things?"

Back in the early Seventies nobody had heard of hang gliding.

Wherever I spoke of it people seemed caught up, often mesmerized. They listened raptly to my tales of exuberant young men launching themselves under kite-like contraptions . . . to accounts of would-be aviators, draping their arms over bamboo frames and running pell-mell down the hill—without engines or tow-lines—until their sails filled with air and their feet no longer touched the ground.

Hang gliding tapped into man's ancient desire to emulate birds. "They really *fly*?" my listeners asked. "Without power?"

"Yes," I said. "Like eagles. But not silently. The plastic sail crackles like laundry flapping in the wind."

"Wow!" they said.

The more they heard, the more the sport emerged as a surreal, even mystical experience. People everywhere seemed fascinated.

It seemed likely that editors would be fascinated too.

FOR YEARS I'D BEEN doing everything all wrong, blithely writing articles about whatever I cared about, my *passion du jour*, then looking for places to send them.

Only later did I learn the truth, that professionals submit articles to magazines only after they've researched back issues. Furthermore, what most editors want is more of what they already have, though with a new twist or slant.

Of *course* I wasn't selling anything. My violin was never in tune with the rest of the orchestra.

STILL, I LUCKED OUT, thanks to the kids.

Guessing that hang gliding would intrigue the editors of a few eclectic magazines, I found a professional photographer and sent out half a dozen illustrated articles.

We didn't wait long. Back came an envelope from United Airlines *Mainliner* magazine. Not my envelope—theirs. As I ripped it open, a check dropped out. I stared at that slip of paper, incredulous, with the same disbelief that often confounds a new Miss America. Not me . . . really me? . . . oh yes, me! Here it was, a check from an editor, a real money-dispensing editor who wanted my piece!

The amount seemed princely, $350. Even without its symbolic value,

$350 was good for the mid-seventies; it would buy you an airplane ticket to Hawaii. But the symbolism was greater than the money, it meant I was finally and honestly a published person: I could write "author" on a nametag.

Our family happened to be traveling to Hawaii on United Airlines the month my article came out, and it was all I could do not to run up and down the aisle of the plane, pointing to the magazine and proclaiming my authorship.

THE SANDBAR HAD SHIFTED and the river poured through. In quick succession I sold five articles on the dazzling new sport of natural, bird-like flight, using a pseudonym so the editors wouldn't know I was writing about my own sons.

After several more sales I dumped out the shoe box and counted the rejection slips: a hundred and twenty seven, more than I'd ever imagined. But that's okay, I thought, this will be the end of them.

It wasn't the end, or even close.

THE YEARS THAT FOLLOWED those early flights were full of magic. Pied pipers that they were, our two sons led the family into a new and different world. A veil dropped behind us and we all vanished and became part of a dreamy, mystical planet, where young men led and parents followed. No longer in charge of our weekends, Rob and I camped beside mountains to watch our boys soar off peaks and gently float through space. We lived daily with awe. We saw their gliders turn and dive and swoop, watched the sun winking off their sails, now made of dacron, heard their names announced over loudspeakers, realized they'd become champions.

Prodded relentlessly by those same sons, we started a business. Before we quite knew what they'd done to us, we were bankrolling their dreams, helping them open a shop so they could manufacture the aluminum and Dacron hang gliders that they envisioned during their hours of silent, spellbinding flight. Rob was the Rockefeller and I was the inexperienced office temp . . . but they were the builders and thinkers, the dreamers.

Our lives were not our own, but we didn't mind; we willingly traded freedom for vicarious excitement.

Until Eric died.

ERIC'S DEATH BROUGHT OUR mystical world crashing down. He was our third son, not a champion but a follower. He'd flown off a mountain in the San Bernardino mountains and made a terrible mistake. Unaware that a three-sixty degree turn in the wrong hands becomes a diving maneuver, he spiraled into the ground and broke his neck.

Rob and I were devastated.

Eric, who sat beside me every day in the office. Gone. Eric, with his wry sense of humor, his sharp insights about the young men we dealt with . . . always looking for a bargain, beguiling me with flashes of wisdom. His chair now empty. I could hardly go there anymore.

"Why did we let him do it?" Rob asked, "why did we let Eric fly?"

"Because he wanted to," I said, trying desperately to understand. "Because he wanted to experience the same thrills as Bobby and Chris. He wanted to see what it was all about . . . getting airborne."

"No, he didn't," said Rob. "He never wanted to fly. He just wanted to be like his brothers."

WARY NOW, OUR FAMILY wrestled with a decision: should we go on with our hang gliding business? Or should we quit everything, the business and the flying?

The agonizing choice, and why decided as we did, forms the heart of a book I wrote over a period of a decade and a half.

It's enough to say here that, yes, we did go on with hang gliding . . . wiser, somewhat less exuberant, with added layers of caution. When we finally stopped once more, three years later, it was because of a second tragedy . . . wholly unforeseen, as unexpected in its way as being run down by horses in the middle of the freeway.

Our oldest son, Bobby, was flying out at Escape Country, making a commercial for Willys Jeep. The filming helicopter chose to steal extra footage, and in the process flew where it wasn't supposed to go. Unaware of where the helicopter had been, Bobby flew into the invisible wake and was blown down and killed.

OUR GRIEF OVER THIS second tragedy was as profound as you'd imagine. Rob was torn apart. Crushed.

When I heard the news, I thought I would die too. Bobby was gone: my heart would surely stop, my breathing would fail. No mother could endure that much pain and survive.

I waited to die. Expected to die. Imagining it would happen any moment, I was vaguely surprised to find myself still on my feet, still able to move. *I can't lose two sons and live.*

Yet it seemed I could.

THE HANG GLIDING YEARS were over. Rob and I and our First-Flyer son, Chris, left our business (which lived on without us), and I went home to write books.

It occurred to me long afterwards that life consists of phases. Our hang gliding phase had jolted to a cruel, unnatural stop . . . though in some ways that phase never ended because the repercussions went on forever.

The next year found me back at my typewriter, digging deep into my psyche as I tried to make sense of all that had happened.

## Chapter Ten

# LESSONS FROM *To Kill a Mockingbird*

FOR ME, WRITING BEGAN again, though with an intensity that hadn't been there before.

The house was quieter now. Among our remaining four children, all but one were immersed in professional schools: our second son, Chris, in medical school; the fourth son, Kenny, in law school; and our daughter away at college. Only the youngest, Kirk, was still at home.

For me, the hang gliding years cried out to be memorialized. There'd been so much excitement, so much drama and triumph—and of course, tragedy. I didn't want to write about the deaths of my sons, only their lives, but inevitably the good and bad parts clung together. As a passionate, perpetual reader, I knew the story was compelling. The elements were all there, like low-hanging fruit, waiting to be plucked from the tree.

Now . . . if only I could figure out how to do it.

Once again I became a student. I drove into the nearby hills, placed my manual typewriter in my lap, and sat with a copy of Harper Lee's *To Kill a Mockingbird* wedged open beside me. For days . . weeks . . months . . I alternately studied and typed.

Yet it was no easy task trying to study someone like Harper Lee—rather like trying to dissect the mechanics of a tornado while you're in it. She's so **good**. When a writer is almost perfect, you can't always tell *why* she's perfect. It's obvious she's using words, plain ordinary English words, but then you can't understand what she's done to them, why her words are magic and yours aren't.... All I can say is, it's an elusive something that spins out of her mind and lands on the page and you can study it all day long and never fully understand what she did.

The same goes for my students. Sometimes, one of them who's been writing decent but rather ordinary stories for years suddenly comes up with something magical. When that happens, neither the student nor I fully understand what occurred that was different, though I always ask, "Did you write this in a kind of daze, did the words just pour out and you really weren't thinking very hard?" and the student always pauses, like a confused puppy with its head cocked, then says Yes, and admits it was effortless.

Which is nuts, because writing, as far as I'm concerned, is very hard work, and the duller the result, the harder you worked to get it. But the brilliant lines, those sparkling bits for which you're ready to throw up your hands and give thanks to heaven, seem to arrive as a surprise, like a crocus in February.

STILL, HARPER LEE TAUGHT me a few basics, which I *could* understand ... such punctuation rules as the need for complete sentences on either side of a semi-colon.

She allowed me to grasp a few subtle tricks that go into non-action scenes: how the story moves forward in dialogue, but the visual images are carried by small, almost un-noticed bits of action that accompany the speech ... and how both work together to create character.

There was the scene near the end of the book, for instance, where the lawyer, Atticus, and the sheriff, Mr. Heck Tate, gather on the front porch to discuss the stabbing death of the vicious Bob Ewell.

As the two men argue in genteel language, the dialogue is interrupted by numerous small acts: Mr. Tate, surprised by a statement from Atticus, "uncrossed his legs and leaned forward." At another dramatic point: "Mr. Tate got up and went to the edge of the porch. He spat into the shrubbery, then thrust his hands into his hip pockets and faced Atticus. 'Like what?' he said."

And still further: "'Nobody's gonna hush anything up, Mr. Finch.' Mr. Tate's voice was quiet, but his boots were planted so solidly on the porch floorboards it seemed that they grew there."

While we readers are paying close attention to the words—to the face-off between two stubborn men—the author makes us subconsciously aware of their movements about the porch, aware even of Mr. Tate's boots. These almost-unnoticed touches form the mortar of the scene. Yet Harper Lee, clever writer that she is, expects us to focus on the dialogue . . . the bricks.

A master at creating character, Lee brings Atticus Finch to life so skillfully we believe we know him. He is revealed not only by what he does, says, and thinks, but by a fourth method, which feels like a slam dunk, the writer's equivalent of reaching into the basketball hoop to deposit your ball. Atticus is made real *by what other characters in the book say about him.*

Harper Lee chooses Miss Maudie, the neighbor across the street, to sum up Atticus's character—supposedly for his children, but mostly for the reader. After Atticus shoots a mad dog, Miss Maudie explains to his son: "If your father's anything, he's civilized in his heart. Marksmanship's a gift of God, a talent . . . I think maybe he put his gun down when he realized that God had given him an unfair advantage over most living things. I guess he decided he wouldn't shoot till he had to, and he had to today."

Later in the story, when Atticus defends an innocent black man in court, Miss Maudie again explains the father to his children: "I simply want to tell you that there are some men in the world who were born to do our unpleasant jobs for us. Your father's one of them. . . . We're so rarely called on to be Christians, but when we are, we've got men like Atticus to go for us."

OVER THE YEARS, HARPER Lee became my idol and her book my mentor. Of all the volumes I've read, which must be in the high hundreds if not thousands, *To Kill a Mockingbird* stands out as one of the few perfect novels.

*One Summer in Between* by Melissa Mather is another. I can't think of many others. *The Past Is Myself,* by Christabel Bielenberg is one of the perfect memoirs.

And here it's time to make an important point: the requirements for novels and gripping memoirs are exactly the same. A memoir must read in every way like a novel, and to the extent that the drama lays itself out in novel format, it will **seem** like a novel. (This is one of those rules that seeps into the subconscious after you've read a lot of both.)

On the other hand, the best fiction always seems wholly believable, as though it could have happened and must have happened ... as though the characters actually lived and continue to live. Classical, enduring fiction grips the reader long after the book is put down. It seems **real**—as real as a memoir. Readers find themselves discussing the people and the events as though they actually existed.

For me, then, the best novels and the best memoirs belong to categories that are indistinguishable from each other. I am only dimly interested in novels without a strong ring of truth. Fast-moving plot alone may keep me reading and reading breathlessly until I reach the end, but then I think, What did I just read? *Who were those people, anyway?* And soon even the plot grows faint and vanishes.

If a novel hangs on plot alone and pays scant attention to character, not much will be left afterwards to think about or care about.

In both novels and memoirs, character is everything.

As I BEGAN WRITING the story about my sons and our family's six dramatic years in hang gliding, the caution about making it read like a novel had already roosted in my subconscious—and in fact, I kept calling my memoir a novel when it wasn't.

But that was only one lesson. Dozens of others presented themselves as I struggled with that book, as I wrote and re-wrote, over and over.

The re-writes piled up—two, three, four ... nine, ten, eleven, so many that I lost track. It was all so difficult and unwieldy that the book went through mammoth stages, as big to me as life itself, but a learning experience all the way.

I started the book in 1978 and finally sold it in 1991, fourteen years in all, longer than it takes a human being to get born and mostly grow up. So many lessons were absorbed and digested during the creation of that book, it became a mammoth treatise on how to write memoirs. As a result, I've accumulated a wealth of material to pass on to others: a whole chapter on Writing Dramatic Scenes (which will be offered next), chapters on Characterization and Plot.

But there was another benefit. Because the book was so long in the making, I received a second, unforeseen gift: I was able to live with my two lost children, Bobby and Eric, fourteen years longer than anyone else.

Chapter Eleven

# DRAMATIC SCENES

LIKE A VACATIONER WHO leaves his suitcase at home, a novel
or memoir won't travel far without some great dramatic scenes.

Dramatic scenes are why readers buy books.

Booklovers wallow in them. Readers like me don't just hope for
them, we lust after them, yearn for them, read madly until we catch
up with them. And then, having found what we're seeking, we read
the scenes over and over, soaking up the drama, letting our feelings
become involved. We relish them more than dramatic scenes in movies,
because on the written page we can slow the scene down and revel in
its individual parts; we can re-read the best lines until we've wrung
out every scintilla of emotion.

These scenes become *ours*, they're part of what we know and feel
about certain characters, but even more, they're part of what we learn
about the world.

You may think I'm exaggerating, but I'm not.

Show me a novel or memoir that's rich in great, dramatic scenes,
and I'll show you a book that becomes a best seller.

SO HOW DO YOU create a dramatic scene?

The first rule is easy. Write and keep writing. You can't do it in a line or two—or even a paragraph or two. A truly dramatic scene takes pages: paragraphs for the build-up, paragraphs for the unveiling, paragraphs for the interplay between characters, paragraphs for the characters' reactions, paragraphs for the resolution.

If this sounds like quite a few pages, it is—for a major scene, fifteen to twenty manuscript pages, at least.

RECENTLY, ONE OF MY long-time students (a very smart man who is also a teacher), submitted a chapter that summed up the end of a several-year period (and many many chapters), in which a decent frontier man, let's call him Jake, had been searching for his kidnapped wife. Jake makes a terrible decision when, at a crucial moment, he decides to track one set of "bad guys" instead of pursuing those who almost surely have absconded with his wife. Having come agonizingly close to getting her back, this foolish Jake realizes the wife might now be lost to him forever.

The whole class waited for inner fireworks . . . a desolate husband raving to others about his terrible mistake . . . a long period of loneliness and frustration . . . hours of agonized pacing across his meadow . . . nights spent alone in his cabin, acutely aware that his life could have been full and rich but now, because of his unthinkable misjudgment, isn't.

What we got from the writer was almost nothing—a sentence, I think. And then he wrote, "Fifteen years later. . . ."

As I finished carrying on in class, beating up on the poor fellow about the enormous hole in his manuscript, he looked at me and asked with a grin, "You mean the word 'regret' wasn't enough?"

We were all still laughing as class adjourned.

NOT ONLY DOES IT take pages to build a dramatic scene, but only with sufficient pages will the reader think to himself, *This is important.* Subconsciously, the reader equates sheer volume of words with significance, guessing, correctly, that if something is said in a line or two, it can't mean much.

Which is why crafty authors work hard to pull excess lines out of minor moments and add as many lines as possible to the great dramatic turning points.

THE SECOND RULE FOR a dramatic scene is that you must have dramatic material: heart-stopping events are required, as exemplified in these five scenes from published books: (a) a "devoted" husband tells his wife he's leaving her for a pregnant girlfriend; (b) the director of the FBI tells a new lawyer his firm is full of crooks and killers; (c) the parents of a hang gliding champion are stonewalled for hours in a hospital, only to learn their son has died; (d) a defeated witness attempts to murder the children of the lawyer who disgraced him; (e) a young girl is lured into a neighbor's underground hideout and raped and murdered.

It's a rare author who doesn't recognize his dramatic moments long before he writes them.

The exception to this caveat is that a truly gifted author can **make** a dramatic moment out of a relatively un-dramatic situation: John Grisham created high drama over a lawyer passing the bar; Melissa Mather, one of my favorite authors, evoked touching drama over a maid losing her bus ticket. So while for most authors the right material is essential, for a few it's not strictly necessary.

Assuming we have most of the ingredients for drama, how do we *make the scene dramatic*?

Dramatic scenes are built by slowing the action, by noting and lingering on all the small events and seemingly insignificant background details that comprise the scene.

Let's say we're creating a dramatic scene about a man and woman flying tandem in a hang gliding competition. Jenny, the girl, is scared speechless. As she stands with Kirk at the top of a mountain, he says, "Jenny, we're next." She nods. Dimly she's aware that cameras are focused on her . . . that a light wind is blowing up the cliff into her face . . . that Kirk has attached her harness and his to the apex of the control bar . . . that someone is asking if they're ready . . . that Kirk is saying, "Now, Jenny!" . . . that her feet are moving, moving, taking her off the cliff.

Jenny feels nothing at first, just emptiness, a sense that the earth has dropped away. Overwhelmed that she's hanging over endless space, she focuses on minutiae: the tightness of the padded harness hugging her ribs, the shiny smoothness of the aluminum control bar, the seams on her gloves. She hears her own voice in her head, a litany that says, "You're alive, Jenny. Others have done this before and lived. You're going to be okay. Breathe. Breathe."

She hears Kirk say, "Look at me, Jenny." She raises her lids and sees him, and it strikes her as incongruous to be looking into the deep blue of his eyes, only inches away, when she'd last seen them a thousand years ago back in some normal kind of world. He asks if she's all right, and she tries to nod, but her mind knows the assurance is a lie. She will not be all right again until they land . . . and then she remembers, groaning to herself, that this will be hours from now.

Her terror continues through most of the flight, until they are forced to land, a dozen pages later, to help another pilot.

This whole scene could be described in one page, but by building the scene slowly, with telling details, the drama is heightened and the importance of the moment magnified.

Similarly, in example (a), drawn from Maeve Binchy's *Tara Road*, the author employs *fourteen pages* to build the drama of an unsuspecting wife jilted by her beloved husband—a man whom we learn, well into a restaurant scene, has a pregnant mistress.

The tension builds slowly, from the moment the wife suggests that they—the couple—ought to have a third baby, cleverly worded by the author so the wife seems to be saying a new baby would be good for the husband. The reader grasps all is not well when the husband says, "How long have you known?"

Still, the wife doesn't catch on when the husband says moments later, "I can't understand why you're so bloody calm!"

The tension builds further as the husband shouts, "Oh God, I don't believe it," and the still-unsuspecting wife tells him to keep his voice down, she doesn't want the whole restaurant to know.

At last, a full page and a half into the scene, the husband admits he's been seeing someone and " . . . we've just discovered she's pregnant." He adds, "We are very happy about it. I was going to tell you next weekend. I thought suddenly that you must have known."

In the following paragraph, note the details that are employed to slow the pace and bring the reader into the wife's grief:
"The noise in the restaurant changed. People's cutlery started to clatter more and bang loudly off people's plates. Glasses tinkled and seemed about to smash. Voices came and went in a roar. The sound of laughter from the tables was very raucous. She could hear his voice from far away. 'Ria. Listen to me, Ree-ah.' She couldn't have said anything. 'I wouldn't have had this happen for the world, it wasn't part of any plan. I wanted us to be . . . I didn't go looking for something like this. . . .' "

And still the scene isn't over. The husband stumbles through apologies and explanations, and the wife's responses are vague and disjointed, hardly more than a word at a time.

Finally she gets up to leave: "She walked unsteadily toward the door of the restaurant while Danny stood helplessly at the table watching her go. But her legs felt weak, and she began to sway. She wasn't going to make the door after all. (The restaurant owner) put down two plates hastily and moved toward her. He caught her just as she fell, and moving swiftly he pulled her into the kitchen."

Some writers might be dazzled by the wealth of extraneous detail like clattering cutlery, tinkling glasses, and raucous laughter, realizing that the reader has been given "reaction time"—low-key moments to respond to the seriousness of the situation.

*In fact, "reaction time" is a major component of all dramatic scenes.*

Most beginning writers would think this much display of grief would be sufficient. But no. The author shows the wife sitting up all night in her evening clothes, shows her questioned by two puzzled children the next morning, and again responding vaguely as though from a faraway planet. Only after many more pages of scenes with concerned friends, with her mother, is the beleaguered wife able to respond with something approaching normalcy.

Fourteen pages. Yet even as the story moves into other, less dramatic realms, the reader is reminded often, though now in a lower key, about the wife's continuing sense of loss.

In each of the above books, dramatic scenes are slowed (and at the same time heightened), by "telling detail" noted within the scene but not strictly necessary for what's going on. Oddly, the reader pays scant attention to this seemingly extraneous material, recognizing subconsciously which details are important and which aren't . . . while deeply affected, nevertheless, by their presence.

Dramatic scenes always imply that the stakes are high for the characters. The outcome matters a lot—and the more it matters to the characters, the more it matters to the reader. Without great importance to someone in the book, there can be no importance to the reader.

Dramatic scenes always build—from smaller events and smaller reactions to larger ones. In general, the highest, most emotional point in a scene comes toward the end. And while the writer can include character reactions to this great moment, he cannot add a last, less important event without producing a sense that the scene "drops off."

An additional, tacked-on event in a dramatic scene, such as characters speaking of something that happened earlier, or a final, trivial happening, pulls the scene down, and is known as "going past the dramatic point."

The problem with going past the dramatic point is that it makes the reader feel deflated and let down. Just as he's responding emotionally to the full impact of the electrifying moment, taking it all in viscerally, he's asked to pay attention to something minor. And he doesn't want to.

When the highest dramatic point is reached, the curtain must go down.

IT IS INTERESTING TO note that George Bernard Shaw, surely one of the world's most gifted playwrights, was also capable of going past the dramatic point. In the last scene of *Major Barbara,* (which I saw twice), the 'Major Barbara' character comes to grips with a final, altered viewpoint, but does so in such a blizzard of words and redundancy of ideas that the audience grows ever more restless. One can literally hear them losing interest.

Seeing it for the second time, I was able to discern the repeated

thoughts that dragged down an anti-climactic last speech, and I ached
to get out my red pen and do some judicious cutting . . . which, of
course, would be the ultimate in nerve.

Ah well. Wouldn't any of us love to create something so enduring,
if a tiny bit flawed.

Some dramatic scenes are mainly confrontational, built
around one character gaining the upper hand over another . . the kind
of scene that I, for one, relish—perhaps because we've all dreamed
of speaking so brilliantly that we are able to put down an adversary
with just the power of words. Confrontational scenes bring out the
Walter Mitty in all of us.

A small note: if the author has a choice between conveying information in narrative or in dialogue, he should choose dialogue, which is
invariably more powerful. My students sometimes run through events
twice—they tell it first in narrative, then again in somebody's speech,
which leaves the dialogue hanging as limp as a luffing sail.

The following is one of my favorite dramatic scenes, a
confrontation between two characters that beautifully illuminates
them both. The book is *One Summer in Between*, the author, Melissa
Mather. The storyline concerns a black girl, Harriet, (the "I" character
in the book) who spends the summer as a nanny for a white Vermont
family, the Daleys. In a twist on conventional stereotypes, Harriet is
beset by prejudices, while the host family is not.

Harriet has just gone to her bedroom and discovered that her bus
ticket home is missing: "'I should never have given her the ticket,' said
Mrs. Daley. 'It wasn't fair to put the responsibility on her.'

"I wished they would make up their minds whether they considered
me a fool or a thief. I rose to my feet and I said, 'Mrs. Daley, I honestly
thought it would be safe where I hid it. Mr. Daley, I swear to God I
did not take that ticket, I am not just pretending it is lost—'

"Mr. Daley thundered, 'Is that what you think we think?'

"I said, 'Why not?'

" 'You really think we think you are planning to cash that ticket
and then tell us you lost it? You think we think you're capable of some

such lowdown, sneaky, conniving maneuver?'

" 'I—I wouldn't be surprised if you thought so,' I said defensively.

" 'Aren't you accustomed to having people take your word for anything?'

" 'No, sir,' I said. 'Not white people.'

" 'Oh, God,' he groaned, 'here we go again. Can't you keep race out of anything? Do you honestly believe, although you've been a member of this household if not of this family for nearly two months now, that neither Mrs. Daley nor I have any idea what kind of a person you are? Do you think because you have a black skin and we have a white skin, we immediately lose all judgment of people?' He stood up. 'You listen to me, Harriet Brown,' he said. 'I don't have any idea where the hell that ticket is, but I know one thing for sure—neither do you.' "

Coming as it does toward the end of the book, this dramatic scene sums up the relationship between the distrustful young girl and the employer-family . . . those wise adults who understand human behavior and motivation so much better than she does.

MOST DRAMATIC SCENES ARE preceded by a lengthy buildup to the big moment:

Using (a) *Tara Road*, once more as an example . . . the author devotes several pages to the wife's thoughts about having a third baby, to her vague concerns that there'd recently been less lovemaking at home, to her anticipation of a lovely meal out with her husband. When the husband finally reveals the truth about his mistress, the reader feels as shocked as if a dump truck had just upended its garbage onto the woman's head.

In example (b), *The Firm*, the biggest dramatic scene in the book involves the director of the FBI (presumably J. Edgar Hoover), telling the protagonist, Mitch, the horrible truth about his law firm. But there's been plenty of buildup. A junior FBI agent has long-since approached Mitch with cautions; Mitch is lured to the big confrontation by an agent who spots him at a tax seminar; the critical meeting takes place—dramatically—near the Vietnam Wall; the weather is icy, as befits the mood of the scene; a disguised agent sits nearby in a wheelchair; Mitch is told that twenty agents guard the area.

It's hard to imagine a single dramatic device that wasn't employed in this preface. And the scene itself consumes twelve dense pages. (Closer to twenty manuscript pages.)

The buildup to example (c), *Higher Than Eagles*, when the parents learn their son has died, also involves a number of small and large precursors: another son was killed three years earlier; the first dire phone call comes to the mother when a cleaning lady is in her office, and the mother is aware both of the woman's concern and her earthy smell; the trip to the hospital involves a strange, suddenly-gloomy sky; the nurse at the admitting desk brutally stonewalls the parents; a priest happens by and the mother asks him to pray; an investigating policeman arrives and gives misleading information; the father is strangely passive, yet suddenly erupts and startles everyone by demanding a neurosurgeon; the doctor who finally emerges from the ER to tell them the truth won't speak to them there but insists the parents follow him to a special room.

The scene and its aftermath take ten printed pages.

In the dramatic scene from the classic *To Kill a Mockingbird*, example (c), Atticus Finch's children are attacked by a deranged maniac. The buildup includes not only the psychological defeat of the would-be killer, Bob Ewell, by Atticus in an earlier trial, the scene itself is preceded by numerous small, dramatic events: the young girl, Scout, is encased in a "ham"—a confining pageant costume; the night is so dark that Scout trips on her way to the pageant; the children speak chillingly of Haints and incantations; starting home after the event, Scout can hardly see, and Jem worries that she might lose her balance; Jem detects a strange noise; Scout and Jem stop repeatedly because they hear someone walking, the soft rustling of trousers.

Harper Lee used ten pages to cover this event.

The final example (e) from *The Lovely Bones*, is about a young girl who is murdered by a neighbor. The author builds the scene with seemingly innocent devices: the girl's parents and the neighbor once discussed the neighbor's flowers; as a mirror to the fatal event, the night is dark and snowy; the neighbor frightens the girl by saying, "Don't let me startle you," the killer offers to show the girl his underground hideaway; since he uses her first name, the girl assumes the neighbor has heard an embarrassing story about her; the killer promises the wary girl that this event will only take a minute; the girl is aware that the man is looking at her strangely; she notices that his glasses are small and round; the girl's ears are freezing and she thinks about the hat tucked in her pocket; as she enters the underground chamber, she senses that escape will be difficult.

This scene consumes ten pages.

IN ALL DRAMATIC SCENES, there are consequences to the high drama. People's lives are changed irrevocably.

Ria, in *Tara Road*, must recast her life and go on without her beloved husband.

Mitch, in *The Firm*, must now choose between his crooked law firm and eventual prison . . . or the FBI and a fatal "accident" at the hands of his colleagues.

The parents, in *Higher Than Eagles*, must decide how to deal with the sport that's now claimed two of their sons.

Atticus Finch, in *To Kill a Mockingbird*, is forced to consider surrendering his son to be tried for murder.

The mother of the murdered girl in *The Lovely Bones* suffers so acutely that she abandons her family.

IT IS CLEAR, THEN, that a dramatic scene must include a sizable buildup—a number of large and small events and fine points that are precursors to the big moment. The dramatic event itself should be so full of important, and even unimportant, detail—some of it minutiae— that it takes a significant number of pages. The aftermath must bring momentous change to all the important characters involved.

FOR YEARS I'VE BEEN prodding my students to write longer, more detail-filled, more affecting dramatic scenes.

For an equal number of years they've responded with one or two page scenes . . . as though they'd reached the absolute limit of what one writer could conjure up for one dramatic event. As though no more was possible.

A few weeks ago, after an impassioned lecture which was almost a dramatic scene in itself, I said to them, "We're going to have a contest here. Anybody who brings me a five-page dramatic scene will get a prize." Five pages weren't nearly enough, of course, but we had to start somewhere.

To my astonishment, half a dozen students took me up on this and brought in five and six-page dramatic scenes, some so detailed and filled with such telling material they were positively astounding. I saw old scenes re-written and raised to new heights of suspense, and new scenes fleshed out with dramatic details that must have taken a great deal of thought.

The rest of the class was as surprised as I was. Though I kept my promise and brought in prizes, the winning students seemed almost indifferent to them, as though tangible rewards of any kind were secondary to their own sense of accomplishment.

This event made me wonder—should I now start adding bribes to my weekly teaching efforts?

In any case, I hope I've finally gotten through to my students that every work of fiction, every memoir, needs at least one major scene, a huge, roaring big scene, and four or five lesser scenes, all designed to make the reader care.

Whatever else you do in your book, if you can lure the reader into emotional involvement, you've made him yours.

## Chapter Twelve

# THEY COULD FLY A BRICK

WHEN I BEGAN WRITING *Higher Than Eagles,* the manuscript had a different title: *They Could Fly a Brick.* At the time I thought the brick idea unique, that it conjured up a nice whacky image of a flying brick with two kids aboard, an absurdity that could be neatly explained within the pages of the book. But the title changed some time afterwards, which left my book with a dandy explanation inside but no title to go with it.

The original name derived from our early days of hang gliding, when a neighbor, aeronautical engineer Leo Pfankuch, once hunkered down with our boys on the blacktop, helping them create hang gliders while he patiently explained the principles of flight. "You know, guys," he said, "when you're trying to get airborne, speed is the key. It's everything. If you got it going fast enough, you could fly a brick."

At the time, Leo was the perfect surrogate father for our five boys, who needed a pilot/father more than a lawyer/father or even a writer/mother . . . because among all of us, only Leo understood aeronautics, and only he remembered the thrill of being a daredevil boy.

THEY COULD FLY A BRICK flew onto the page quickly, maybe in four or five months. I don't remember struggling. But that was because I didn't know much, so there was nothing to struggle *about*. Fresh from my studies of Harper Lee's *Mockingbird* I wrote with zest and a wholly unwarranted self-confidence, assuming that the magic I'd tried so hard to absorb would just naturally flow onto my pages. For a while, I believed I'd written something wonderful. Or if not wonderful, at least creditable.

The rest of the world didn't think so.

My best friend, Patty Teal, just then starting her career as a literary agent, faithfully sent out *The Brick,* with dismal results. Nobody gave us a nibble—or even an encouraging comment. The rejections piled up so relentlessly the book began to feel like a loser. As with other new artists, my sense of worth faded with stunning speed; all those outside critics must be right.

Only one solution came to mind: start over.

I WAS WELL INTO the first revision, now titled, *An Eagle is Down,* when I attended a writer's party and found myself giddily describing my memoir to a sophisticated agent. For awhile, as I carried on with my usual over-the-top enthusiasm, I imagined I held her attention. Encouraged by her lively expression, I related a few dramatic events, like our sons' unimaginable glider-to-glider jacket transfer out over the Pacific ocean . . . and how, on another occasion, one of them came from behind to become the first United States hang gliding champion.

Abruptly her expression changed. In one of those fleeting moments of self knowledge, I grasped that I'd badly misread her. Still, I wasn't prepared for the knife she actually hurled at me. In the coldest possible tones she said, "You'll never sell that book."

My face flamed up. My breath whooshed out and I looked away, so mortified I could hardly speak. Finally I managed to squeak in a faint imitation of my own voice, "Why not?"

"It's not the kind of story people want to read."

Her bluntness stopped me again. But then stubbornness took over, abetted by flash-by images of first-person dramas I'd read over the years. "But they do!" I cried, knowing she was mistaken. "I find books like this everywhere. The *Reader's Digest* condensed books has one or two personal-experience stories every month. They're always the first ones I read!"

She gave me a pitying look, the insect who'd had the audacity to argue. "People are sick of those disease-of-the-month books."

I just stared at her. Something inside rebelled, blossomed into scorn, then fury. I hated her supercilious attitude, her arrogance. No, more, I hated her personally. She was worse than arrogant, she didn't know what she was talking about. I knew more than she did and vowed that I'd prove it. Mine was a good story, it had all the elements, suspense, humor, moments of great triumph and, God help us, tragedy. All it needed was a writer good enough to make it come to life.

But she didn't know whether I was good enough or not; she had no inkling of what I could or couldn't do. She'd put me down with a rare brand of snobbishness, the snooty agent dismissing my subject as not worth anyone's effort. I thought her a know-all who knew very little.

It was a pivotal moment, an epiphany.

Some day, somehow, I'd come back with a published book.

Her unintended motivation carried me for years. Each time I considered quitting, I thought of her.

That agent's role in my life endures to this day, shimmers before my eyes as a kind of beacon. Her influence amazes me—how far one can travel on anger and a pent-up desire to prove oneself right.

PATTY TEAL SENT OUT the revision. With still no success, no hint that the story was any better, I had to re-think it once more.

For the first time since my Stanford days, it occurred to me that I needed help, someone professional with sharper insights than mine. It came as another startling self-revelation—that even after all those hours of studying *Mockingbird*, there might be something—a few little things—about words and their organization that I still didn't know. (Now that I really do understand some principles of writing, I'm fairly humble and willing to admit that I get surprised by the difficulty of the craft constantly, almost every day.)

I asked Patty, "Who should I show this to?"

"You might try Pat Kubis," she said. "She teaches Creative Writing at Orange Coast College. I don't know her personally, but I hear she's a gifted teacher."

She was. She's also a good friend now, and a writing colleague, but back then she was just this awesome teacher whom I paid to critique my manuscript.

"The story slows in the middle," Kubis reported back. "From pages 150 to 225 it doesn't move. You may think all those details about your business are fascinating, and I'm sure they were to you, but the reader doesn't care."

Whatever else she said in her analysis, which was two pages long and included a few compliments, I no longer remember. But her comments about the core of my book and how too much of it focused on my attempts to manage a business that was more Boys Town than commerce, forced me to re-think my story. Maybe the premise was off. Or the focus. Maybe she was right, that nobody cared about the endless struggles and comic aspects of an inept mother trying to run a hang gliding business.

Well, I thought, if the reader doesn't care about a business, how about a person?

But which person? Who in our family changed the most as a result of the hang gliding? Who should the camera be looking at?

The answer came suddenly. Our oldest son. Bobby!

If a choice had to be made, he was the family member who started in one place and eventually arrived at another. Bobby was our problem child, yet he was the son who grew remarkably, who "found" himself in a sport.

Pat Kubis suggested tactfully that I might benefit from taking her class.

*I really don't need this, I thought, not me, the accomplished writer who's already sold some magazine articles.* I sat down that first day in class and pretended I was just as much a beginner as everyone else.

Actually, I was. In some ways, I was worse than most beginners, because I was secretly cocky—yet so far removed from real professionalism I didn't yet know how much I didn't know.

Pat asked each of us, "What is your story about? Describe it to me in one sentence," which is the same question I now ask my students.

If we couldn't answer that question, she said, we weren't ready to write.

I quickly learned that a story can never be amorphous, it can't be about "this and that." If I, the writer, didn't know where my tale was going or what it was about, the reader wouldn't know either—or care. That one-sentence summary became my most important single insight.

To the extent that I was able to describe my memoir in one sentence, I grasped suddenly that I'd be on a clear, well-defined track, like a train that's going someplace.

So I worked on it quite a bit and finally came up with my one-sentence synopsis. "This is the story of a disturbed boy who fought his asthma and fought his family, but found himself in the sport of hang gliding."

Right then the train started to roll.

The decision to make the book Bobby's story was critical, the first and single most important turning point in my fourteen-year effort. Once I'd chosen Bobby, each scene required analysis: what does this have to do with our oldest son? How did this event influence, mark, or change him? How does this scene move the story toward its conclusion?

I imagined I was almost there; I'd outwitted the papa troll and made it over the bridge.

I had no idea there were still so many other trolls, each one formidable, still waiting.


LATE IN THE SECOND rejection cycle, an editor at Prentice-Hall made an offhand comment in his refusal letter that changed my career markedly, turning me from simple memoir writer to perpetual genre hopper.

"They sent me your manuscript," Saul Cohen wrote, "because they know I'm doing a series on unpowered flight. Unfortunately. . . . "

Though I dismissed the comment, my agent didn't. Always the wise opportunist, Patty Teal suggested, "Why don't you offer to write a different book for him?"

The idea didn't interest me. "I don't know, Patty. I'm doing my family story and. . . . "

"At least try," she said. "Write him a letter and ask. What have you got to lose?"

She pushed me so hard I thought about it. What *did* I have to lose? "Well. I suppose I could."

Instead of a letter, I went further and sent Saul Cohen a telegram. "At my agent's prodding," I wrote, "I offer myself as an expert to write a fiction or non-fiction book on hang gliding. Qualifications include. . . ." The list that followed made me sound like an authority.

When Saul Cohen didn't respond the next day, I assumed he wasn't interested.

To my surprise, four days later he called. His voice was dry and businesslike. "I think a woman writing a non-fiction book on hang gliding might be an interesting idea," he said.

My heart started to thump; I imagined he could hear it long distance. Trying to sound cool, I said lightly, "Oh good," or something equally brilliant.

He said, "Why don't you send me a proposal?"

"Oh . . . sure. I'll be glad to send you a proposal, Mr. Cohen. I'll get it off right away."

"No rush," he said.

The minute we hung up, I called Patty. She's never made me feel stupid, so I just blurted it out. "What's a proposal?"

QUITE A FEW YEARS later, I learned how to write a non-fiction book proposal, and the next chapter describes in detail how it's done.

But at the time I bluffed like a fool and committed myself blindly to a task for which I was clueless.

Chapter Thirteen

# Writing the Non-Fiction Book Proposal

THE GOOD NEWS ABOUT nonfiction is that it's easier to sell than fiction.

The second, the really spectacular, good news is that you can sell it without writing the whole damnfangled book. You can write a little piece of it, the best little piece it's possible to write, of course, but a mere smidgeon nonetheless, and if you're clever and you really do have enough ideas for an entire book and if it's a topic people care about, editors will offer you a contract on the basis of sixty or so pages. And they'll give you money up front.

Now when you sit down to write, you're no longer typing on a hope and a prayer.

*The work is already sold*!

(This is not always as wonderful as it sounds. Suddenly you've taken on pressure; you've acquired an editor who offers money, but also a deadline—and now, sooner than you might want, he expects you to produce an entire book.)

As always with any selling tool, you infuse your non-fiction book proposal with attitude: the pages must ring with confidence and understated enthusiasm.

Think of your proposal as a grabber. A teaser. Think of it as a coming attraction in the movie theaters, or an attention-grabbing newspaper headline.

BASICALLY, YOU CREATE THIRTY to sixty double-spaced pages which will convince an editor that (a) you have a hot topic, (b) you are an expert in the field and have plenty to say, (c) you know how to write, (d) you've thought it through, and (e) ten other people haven't already written the same book.

Such an approach is possible for a simple reason: publishers have found that nonfiction books from unknown authors sell reasonably well—in small numbers, perhaps, but they do sell and they do make a profit—as long as the subject is compelling and the title a "grabber."

Conversely, memoirs and works of fiction from unknowns are always a gamble. While the occasional first novel or non-celebrity memoir may strike that lucky gold vein and send back tram loads of profit, too many such attempts from unknowns simply go unnoticed. So publishers are loathe to take a chance on manuscripts that, all too often, fail to pay back their own editing and printing costs.

YOUR BOOK PROPOSAL CONTAINS seven basic parts: 1) **Hook** 2) **First Chapter** 3) **Chapter Outline** 4) **Description of Target Audience** 5) **Marketing Plan** (promotion) 6) **List Of Competing Books** 7) **Author Qualifications**.

Let's begin with the **Hook**. How do you interest an editor in your topic? What is there about your project that says, Buy Me?

Let's pretend that you're about to write a new diet book—a perpetually hot topic, since so many Americans are overweight and nearly all would rather be thin and most would buy anything, a purple book with raised yellow spots, if they thought it could influence their waistlines.

As a start, your book would need a new approach, something radically different, since diet books have been blowing across the landscape like detritus for years. But let's say you are a doctor and have discovered that certain combinations of foods will magically raise a dieter's metabolism (which is what we all want, isn't it?)

The **Hook** is clear. The first couple of sentences would read something like, "Nobody wants to be fat. Now, for the first time in modern history, nobody **needs** to be fat. It's finally possible that, by eating ordinary foods in extraordinary combinations, people in all weight ranges, even the morbidly obese, can raise their metabolisms to new, fat-burning levels."

Obviously this news can be stated in a dozen different ways, all dramatic. But it's best to be as direct and as simple as possible.

The next paragraph would add detail to the enticing opening: what kinds of foods you, the author, are talking about, a summary of expected weight losses, a rehash of the years of observation and study that contributed to these conclusions.

Because a magical claim like this would create skepticism in any editor, you'd need to include side pages of statistical evidence to validate your claim—charts, data, statistics, study results, anything that would prove your results are backed up by good science. No publisher wants to be taken in by a fraudulent author. On the other hand, every editor yearns to be the guiding hand behind a new, hundred-thousand-copy book.

**First Chapter:**

The opening chapter serves several purposes. It offers proof that the author knows how to write. It lays out the overall premise and demonstrates persuasiveness. It reveals the author's winning personality (or lack thereof).

Will you, the doctor, appeal to the average reader? Can you make a convincing case? Will this first chapter entice readers and editors to turn the pages?

Here is where the author puts on a full court press. The first chapter cannot be considered ready until a number of impartial readers declare it utterly convincing.

**Chapter Outline:**

Without writing an entire book, it's difficult to know *exactly* what the text will cover, but if you've been thinking about this project for some time, you'll have ideas about chapter topics. Here's where you do your organizing, your logical presentation of assorted facts. The manuscript will contain a minimum of eight chapters, but probably more.

In the fewest words possible, include a summary of topics covered in each chapter. This can be done in either narrative or outline format . . . but remember, its only purpose is to convince an editor that you do have enough material to fill a book.

WITH A UNIQUE AND convincing **Hook**, a great **First Chapter**, and proof that there's enough *material for many chapters*, you've fulfilled the most difficult requirements of a nonfiction proposal.

The rest is the frosting that the editor needs to take to his committee— to convince others in the publishing house that not only do you have a well-written and much-needed project, but your promotion efforts will give it a good chance of success.

NOW ON TO MARKETING—THE second half of your proposal.

**Target Audience:**

In this section you will list the readers for your book. Since it's a diet book, the audience is pretty obvious. (Big).

**Promotion:**

Here you discuss your ideas for selling the finished book, which might include speeches to certain target groups such as Overeaters Anonymous, a variety of women's groups like AAUW and Soroptomist, and groups of MDs who deal with obesity. You might run a provocative ad in *Radio-TV Interview Report*\*, create a press kit\*\*, and hire a publicist. Here is where you state that you are experienced and comfortable giving talks before large audiences.

**Competing Books:**

Before a publisher will offer a contract for a book, he must be sure that your manuscript is not just a rehash of other published works. You will save your editor time and add a tone of professionalism by including a list of similar texts—none of which, however, is exactly like yours. Amazon.com is a good place to do book research, and might even convince you all over again that no other book offers the same premise, or data even close to yours. Providing a list of competing books, and a one-sentence summary of how each is dissimilar, offers proof to the publisher that you've done your homework.

**Author Qualifications:**

This is your bio, your detailed description of you, the author . . . of your past writing experiences, your history in the diet field, your years of observations and first-hand experiences with your subject. This is the page that should convince an editor that you, and only you, are qualified to write this diet book.

**Title:**

One last selling tool would be a fantastic, grabber title. Good luck. Titles are never easy; catchy names can soak up a lot of brainstorming. If you've already dreamed up a great title, your project will have ten times the appeal of the proposal that arrives on a publisher's doorstep without one.

But not to worry. If you haven't conjured up that last bit of magic, the sparkling title, one way or another you and your publisher will find a way to do it.

THE DIET BOOK PROPOSAL written by a doctor may be an unfair example, because it's so much easier to describe than other nonfiction proposals.

So let's switch to another kind of nonfiction. How about a book by a woman who's been raped and has spent years talking to other rape victims, gathering stories, and seeking solutions?

What if you are that woman and you have no formal degrees in your subject, no "qualifications" except the obvious one . . . but you do have a wealth of ideas accumulated from listening to other preyed-upon women, from discussions with law enforcement officials, and from your own attempts to make your life safer. Can you develop a book proposal that would be taken seriously?

Yes, you can.

Your hook comes ready made: in the first paragraphs you would describe, briefly, the traumatic event itself. "I was sound asleep when my bedroom window began opening. I awoke to a small squeak and the soft sound of shoes crossing my bedroom carpet. The next thing I knew a hand jerked back my blankets. I screamed and the hand slammed against my mouth."

In subsequent paragraphs, you'd enumerate the rape's long-lasting emotional, perhaps crippling, effects on your life.

Further paragraphs would summarize your very real attempts, not only to make your own life better and safer, but your various efforts to help other women work through their deep psychological traumas. You might mention that in talking to so many victims you've learned that rape is much more prevalent than you once thought—experts estimate maybe ten percent of all women—and you've come to believe that rape can happen to anyone, anywhere.

You might mention that you've acquired X number of personal stories—from letters and first-hand accounts—and will devote chapters to them, then analyze and summarize them to make the following points about rape: (a) age is no determiner (b) women's backgrounds can vary wildly (c) the victim's behavior and/or sexy clothing is not a factor (d) time of day, setting, home or work conditions, can be as diverse as the women themselves.

AS A RAPE VICTIM without formal credentials, you'll have to enlist other "authorities" to help give the proposal credibility. Among listed chapters might be references to policemen, rape counselors, centers for rape victims . . . plus quotes from judges, psychiatrists, special task forces . . . anyone who deals with rape professionally.

Final chapters will be devoted to "answers": ways of becoming whole psychologically, and useful steps for making sure one doesn't become a target in the first place.

If the proposal is written with passion, expertise, and good English, and includes convincing solutions for the problem, it should have genuine editor appeal.

ANY NONFICTION PROPOSAL IS enhanced if the author can promise that a "big name" in her field has agreed to write an introduction—especially if the name is illustrious enough to be featured on the book's jacket.

It helps, too, if the author can find an agent to represent her. Not only will the agent know the best editors to approach, but presumably she'll be able to assure these professionals that the author will make a good salesman for the book—that she is a fluent speaker, believable, and enthusiastic.

ALTHOUGH I RECENTLY SOLD a book on the basis of a formal, nonfiction proposal (and years ago sold another, my first book ever, on a proposal that was such a wild, unprofessional bluff I can't believe it was taken seriously), if I had either of them to do over I'd make substantial changes. Instead of the 100, double-spaced pages I submitted the last time, I'd try to stay under sixty, remembering that editors are harried and overworked and might react faster to a shorter submission. If you can't convince someone in sixty pages, you'll likely do no better in twice the length.

I'd organize my proposal as I've suggested here—presenting every detail about the book itself first, and all the marketing strategies second . . . with the rationale that an editor has to be intrigued by the contents of a book before he'll care a penny's worth about how it's promoted.

I'd envision my proposal as a pyramid . . . with the most captivating elements at the peak, and working downward to myriad foundation details—the way most good newspaper stories are presented.

I'd tell myself repeatedly: you don't start with the ordinary stuff, you begin with the grabbers.

But isn't that the way with all writing?

*FOR THOSE WHO'VE NEVER seen a copy of *Radio-TV Interview Report*, it's a magazine full of catchy ads about authors and speakers, with headlines so provocative they're nearly irresistible.

Examples, from a recent copy of the magazine:

**"Are People Getting Weirder? Ask this psychologist."**

**"Are You Headed for Job Burnout? 5 signs you might be missing."**

**"Is Your Clean Home Making Your Family Sick?"**

**"2 Million Americans Will Divorce this Year. This Relationship Expert Says Most People Marry the Wrong Person."**

**"Former Member of WWII's Patton's Raiders Asks . . . Does**

**America Still Have What It Takes To Fight For Freedom?"
"Why Big-Money Donors Really Own the White House."
"Why More Americans Should Carry Guns."**
Most of us would find it difficult to create headlines this enticing, but luckily the editors are happy to help.

Radio and television hosts regularly choose speakers from among these blurbs . . . and in fact, for my latest book, that magazine brought me well over 50 interviews.

*Radio and TV Interview Report* also has a website: *http://www.rtironline.com/* free to view the headlines and links.

**For writers who've never** created a press kit, it's a simple cardboard folder with the book's cover pasted to the outside, and the two inside flaps filled with the following:

- A News Release about the book
- Sample questions to be asked by the media
- A Glossy Author Photo
- An Author Bio
- Favorable Reviews of the book
- A Pitch Letter inviting television/radio interviews
- The Author's Book Tour Itinerary

The insert sheets are multi-colored and often cleverly cut to varied lengths, so the headline portion of each sheet can be seen at a glance.

## Chapter Fourteen

# THE ACCIDENTAL BOOK

MY FIRST BOOK PROPOSAL, the one that actually sold my first published volume, was a bluff. Having only the vaguest idea (even after talking to Patty), I wrote part of a first chapter, three pages only, because at the moment three pages covered everything I could conjure up. For the rest I created lists.

After eight years of immersion in the heady world of hang gliding, producing lists was easy: all the contests our kids had won (several dozen); all the out-of-state sites at which I'd watched hang gliding; all the famous people I knew in the sport (Paul MacCready, creator of the Gossamer Albatross; and Francis Rogallo, designer of the Rogallo Wing); all the hang gliding books in my library; all the forthcoming contests; all the world-records; all the feature films (Twentieth-Century Fox's *Skyriders*), and low budget documentaries (literally dozens).

I also began hauling out articles to prove my writing skills and, over-the-top as usual, might have sent Saul Cohen everything I'd ever committed to paper.

"You **can't** do that," Patty said. "Really, Maralys. Not ten articles. One or two. Maybe just one."

Heat slid up my face. What had I been *thinking?*

"Have you started the body of the proposal?"

"I've got some ideas."

I had no ideas.

Even as I bluffed, I knew my attempt was flimsy, that Saul Cohen would see the emperor had no clothes. It certainly wasn't the outline for a book and didn't pretend to be. But it was all I could scrape together. I kept reminding myself I'd been caught off guard, that I was a memoir writer who'd never intended to write a general nonfiction in the first place.

Saul Cohen would have it on his desk soon, and if logic counted for anything, after one glance he'd wriggle off the hook and swim back to sea.

So much for Prentice-Hall. Somehow the thought didn't disturb me. Hey, I was used to rejections, had enough now to overflow my shoebox.

SAUL COHEN DIDN'T SIT on the proposal long. Within a week he'd contacted my agent offering her a contract, with an advance of ten thousand dollars.

Ten thousand dollars!

Patty might not have been speechless, but I certainly was. Ten thousand dollars for a book about which I hadn't a clue! A book that, except for the confluence of a few scattered circumstances, I'd never intended to write. For that kind of money he'd want something thick and pagey; he'd expect a virtual encyclopedia of hang gliding.

Somehow, with minimal effort, I'd managed to catch a buffalo in a mousetrap.

OVER THE NEXT FEW days, my attitude changed. Now that a contract was actually in the works, I lightened up and was thrilled, as excited as if the plan had been set into motion deliberately. I was, after all, only minimally published and a book was a book was a book. With the naiveté of the mostly-rejected, I imagined that a first book, any book at all, was a master key that would unlock all future publishing doors. I really believed this. From now on, I'd sell everything that left my typewriter. "You understand I've published a book," I'd say, and casually toss my cape over my shoulder, and the editor's eyes would light up and she'd ask, grabbing for my manuscript, "What would it take to make you happy?"

(An editor actually said that once, many years and many books later, when I was trying to get him to budge from a paltry advance of five thousand dollars. Finally what made me happy was a three-book contract and a lot more money.)

GOD MUST PROTECT NOVICE writers. If He didn't, when we learned the truth about publishing, we'd all fling ourselves out of ten-story windows.

THE EARLY BLUFFING HADN'T been a problem. But something else was.

Soon after the contract arrived I saw in the future an un-climbable mountain. I'd have to start the book with the history of unpowered flight, about which I knew nothing. Not just a little nothing, but a lot of nothing.

How do you begin a book when you're staring at a precipice without handholds, and you know you've got to surmount it before you can move on? How do you sound like an expert on a topic about which you are clueless?

The more I thought about that part, the more I worried. Nobody wants to come off in print sounding like an idiot, but that's where this was headed.

For a few nights I woke at 3:00 a.m., wondering why I'd accepted a contract that obligated me to make a fool of myself in front of the whole aviation community. Surely, I thought, the REAL experts will follow the yellow brick road to the end and find me sitting Oz-like on my make-believe throne, a little fraud of a person who is all pretense and no facts.

I seemed to have a choice . . . send back the contract or continue bluffing.

There was no decent way out except to write the book.

WHERE TO START?

Gil Dodgen, the editor of *Hang Gliding Magazine*, who, like me, had jumped into a job he didn't know, offered critical advice. "If you don't know what to do first," he said, "do something. The rest will come to you."

The only "something" I could think of was to head for the nearest library, hoping a few hang gliding authors had included information about early, unpowered flight.

But wait . . . what was I thinking? *All* early flight was unpowered. Until the Wright brothers came along to smog up the landscape with engines, every attempt to get airborne was birdlike and motorless, which made the history of hang gliding essentially the same as the history of all modern aviation. If you thought about it, hang gliding was nothing more than an exhilarating, camera-ready, re-invention of an earlier mode of flight.

Well. This might be okay!

With that I pored through books, and after a while famous would-be aviators like Leonardo Da Vinci, and George Cayley, and the Lilienthal brothers, and Pilcher, and the Montgomery brothers, came to life and creaked their way off the pages to tell me their stories.

One day I finished scribbling notes, and thought, *I don't need these anymore . . . I am an expert*!

My favorite tale concerns the final aviation escapade of an Englishman, Sir George Cayley, who was born about 1800, and who secretly tinkered with flight for nearly seventy years, creating surprisingly advanced sketches of aeronautical parts like curved wings and propellers.

Most of Cayley's odd-looking craft were reputed to have flown unmanned or with someone else at the helm, but it's difficult, judging from his sketches, to imagine some of them flying under any conditions—unless it's possible to become airborne in a small wheelbarrow with four windmills and two propellers.

Residents of Brompton, England, still relish the final George Cayley story. When he was eighty, immortality arrived in the form of a remarkable flying machine which Cayley was clearly too old to test-fly himself. Instead, he persuaded his coachman to take the craft to a nearby cliff overlooking a valley.

How Cayley cajoled the poor fellow into becoming a test pilot will never be known. In any event the coachman duly departed the cliff attached to Cayley's contraption, became airborne, and cleared the hedgerows of Brompton for about fifteen hundred feet. At the end he crashed, demolishing the machine. With that he clambered out of the wreck, looked back over his path of glide, and realized with horror where'd he'd been.

Deciding one such event was enough, he approached Cayley and formally surrendered his coachman's cap. "I was engaged to drive," he said stiffly, "not fly."

IT TURNED OUT THAT Saul Cohen understood nonfiction book proposals better than I did. All those lists transformed themselves into good, readable text. I used every one. In fact it's hard to imagine how I'd have written the book without making the lists first.

Without the need for plot, characterization, scenes, conflict, theme, setting, or dramatic structure, the writing of the Prentice-Hall book was a gentle process, a matter of letting words flow.

I kept thinking how much easier it was than memoir-writing, where you're trying to keep seven or eight tasks in the air at once, like juggling oranges, and if one of them gets away and splats on the ground, they all fall, and you've got a mess, and it's impossible to start again until you clean up and get the oranges re-launched.

Oh sure, for the Prentice-Hall book I had to craft decent sentences. But beyond that I was required only to be organized, factually correct and, God willing, interesting.

WHILE THE WRITING ITSELF was easy, the corollary tasks made it the world's longest term paper.

Nobody told me that writing a comprehensive nonfiction comes with a hundred extra chores—a surprise that begins to feel like you've stepped on the wrong bunch of leaves and fallen into a pit.

The added jobs kept falling in on top of me: first I was scrambling for photos, then photographers, then captions, then text to tie them to . . . all the while keeping the lot organized so Prentice-Hall could make sense of it.

The same went for quotes from magazines and books, quotes from live people, and material from places like the Smithsonian Institution. And hanging above all those chores, like tablets handed down from On High, were Saul Cohen's admonitions that every borrowed sentence, every treasured photo must be accompanied by a written permission. You couldn't just throw presents under the tree without tags.

The permissions were the worst. If someone breathed on the book, Prentice-Hall required permission to use it.

Later came thank-you notes. By the end I'd written more words in the form of letters than for the book itself.

UNWIELDY AS IT WAS, the project came with attractions. My son, Chris, the First U.S. Champion, wrote a 40-page section called, *How To Fly.* His wife, Betty-Jo Wills, tirelessly compiled an enormous appendix called *The Hang Glider Pilot's Baedeker.* My husband, Rob, as Chairman of the Accident Review Board, wrote a lengthy introduction.

It felt like we were all down in the pit together.

Saul Cohen named the Book, *Manbirds: Hang Gliders and Hang Gliding,* and the next year, Library Journal listed *Manbirds* as one of the 100-best books in Science and Technology.

Astonishing revelation # 1. *Manbirds* never became the key that unlocked even one publishing door. But I was glad I'd made the effort because now I was a published book author with full bragging rights.

I'd learned a great deal about writing nonfiction books, most of which will be covered in the next chapter.

I was also free to genre-hop back to my other book and pick up where I'd left off, which would of course get written fast and easily.

Of course.

Chapter Fifteen

# WRITING NONFICTION BOOKS

*I'M NOT SURE WHEN we began to lose our youngest son.*
*I hear him as he is now when he calls home from state prison—at*
*thirty-seven, flat, depressed, cynical and suspicious—and the thought*
*comes to me, as it has so often, that we **can't** let him fade away on us,*
*we have to find a way to rescue him. We can't, we simply can't lose*
*another son.*
*Yet Kirk is slipping away. And we don't know how to stop him.*
*With all our supposed brains, with all the solutions we've managed*
*to find to other problems, we've so far had none for this one.*

THUS BEGINS THE FIRST chapter of my nonfiction book,
*Save My Son.* Clearly a sad and personal beginning for what is mostly
an impersonal book on the U.S. criminal justice system's approach
to addiction.

This passage is quoted as an example of the kind of beginning
needed even for nonfiction books—paragraphs that turn into "grabber" first pages.

Nonfictions may be easier to write than their fictional counterparts,
but that first page is still the literary equivalent of trying to leap ten
feet from a standing start. It still demands a lively opener that excites

the reader and pulls him along. It's still a task without definitions, still hard to get exactly right.

The difference between first pages in nonfiction books and fiction is that the nonfiction has a lighter burden to carry. There is no story requirement here, no need to plant seeds that presage character, plot, or conflict—or any of the tricky themes that will play out in future chapters. You can be straightforward in nonfiction. Interesting and gripping, always. But not necessarily devious.

As in magazine articles, the best beginnings for nonfiction books focus on people, and usually on a particular person. Any human interest story that deals with the theme or purpose of your book is a good way to start. The best nonfiction books drag us in by making us care about someone—about a bag lady's rise out of abject poverty, about cancer victim Lance Armstrong winning the Grand Prix, about a mother finding triumph for her crippled child, about four competitors in a walking race across Australia. You can never go wrong approaching your subject dramatically in terms of one tragic or triumphant individual.

Irving Stone's opening lines in his historical text, *Men to Match My Mountains*, exemplify the kind of start we're all looking for: "Captain John Augustus Sutter had cause to be concerned. Had he fled the imminence of a Swiss debtors' prison only to end in a political prison in California? And just at the moment when his colony here in the Sacramento Valley, launched in the teeth of harrowing hardships, was about to be realized?"

Jon Krakauer's first page in his adventure saga, *Into Thin Air*, provides an equally compelling start to a serious nonfiction: "Straddling the top of the world, one foot in China and the other in Nepal, I cleared the ice from my oxygen mask, hunched a shoulder against the wind, and stared absently down at the vastness of Tibet. I understood on some dim, detached level that the sweep of earth between my feet was a spectacular sight. I'd been fantasizing about this moment, and the release of emotion that would accompany it, for many months. But now that I was finally here, actually standing on the summit of Mount Everest, I just couldn't summon the energy to care."

Then there's the start to Columnist Jack Smith's book, *Eternally*

*Yours*, also a personal close-up, but of an entirely different sort: "I used to spend hours in my youth imagining romantic names for myself, names that evoked my character, or the character I hoped to have: Quentin Randolph, Fulton Duffield, Marshall Kent, Lancelot Grant, Morgan Cortright. I would write them down and roll them about on my tongue. Jack Smith is something of an embarrassment, being the most common name in the English-speaking world. I actually don't mind its being common, since I have no pretensions; but I do mind being accused of having made it up to conceal my true identity—as if I had no more imagination than that."

Michael Korda's *Another Life*, a nonfiction about the publishing industry, begins with Korda's thoughts on his own early life. "I was twenty-three before it occurred to me that my future might not lie in the movie business.

"Until then, I had always taken it for granted that I would follow in my family's footsteps sooner or later. . . . "

And last, in the book *Monster*, John Gregory Dunne begins his expose about screen writing as follows: "In the spring of 1988, my wife, Joan Didion, and I were approached about writing a screenplay based on a book by Alanna Nash called *Golden Girl*, a biography of the late network correspondent and anchorwoman Jessica Savitch. In the spring of 1996, the motion picture made from our screenplay, now called *Up Close and Personal*, and no longer about Jessica Savitch, was released. This is a story about the making of that movie, about the reasons it took eight years to get it made, about Hollywood, about the writer's life, and finally about mortality and its discontents."

IN EACH OF MY nonfiction books, I began with a close-up on an individual . . . and further paragraphs in the opening of *Save My Son*, describe the frosty December night our addicted son appeared at the front door—bedraggled, desperate, lonely, having been forced to walk seven miles in the cold after he was released from jail.

Whatever your theme, whatever your mission in writing a nonfiction book, it is worth spending the energy to begin your first chapter homing in on an individual whose story has book-wide relevance.

NONFICTION BOOKS, EVEN THOSE written with substantial author expertise, often involve research. Later, Chapters 21 and 23 deal with research extensively, but it's enough to say now that doing research bestows a sense of authenticity on your efforts, making you feel like you've brought in a second opinion. The outside world confirms your viewpoint.

Research is dependably gratifying. All you need say over the phone or anywhere else, is, "I'm writing a book, and I need to know ... " to ensure that you'll get all the information you want and probably more besides. People really do expend astonishing amounts of energy trying to supply information to writers—especially people in Public Relations.

Not only do most large organizations have a PR department, but their officers are like tooth fairies in their eagerness to please the public.

Even in such a formal environment as the Norfolk Naval Base in Norfolk, Virginia, a public relations officer was willing to offer details about the Admiral's office (blue carpet, hanging wall plagues commemorating the Admiral's prior assignments), so many specifics I felt I'd been there. Even years later, it seems I must have visited the site.

WHEREAS THE UNDERLYING PURPOSE of fiction and most memoirs is entertainment and escape, the purpose of nonfiction is to inform and edify ... sometimes to offer a new slant on an old subject ... often to persuade. Yet increasingly, even the nonfiction reader seeks to be entertained.

A big nebulous fog arises in a reader's mind when an author loses track of why he's writing the book.

A book invariably starts to sink when the author has no clear idea of his purpose. A few students in my class are writing historical novels, and those that see their mission as mostly informational lose their novelist's perspective and produce scenes that are neither dramatic nor really enlightening. . . .

Conversely, a nonfiction writer hoping to convey a message dares not bog down in made-up material, because the one element readers look for in nonfiction is Truth. Readers of nonfiction expect to be educated, they expect to revel in facts that can be verified and in viewpoints backed up by proof. Like my husband, Rob, most want knowledge—ever more of it, and always for its own sake.

Rob, a dedicated nonfiction reader, worships facts and hoards them in his brain the way misers tuck away small bits of string. He dismisses most fiction as "fairy tales," and the way he says "Oh, that's *fiction*," it comes off as a dirty word.

The nonfiction writer is obligated, therefore, to be on an endless quest for truth, because veracity is what readers expect.

NONFICTION AUTHORS SOMETIMES ASK how much information they can "steal" from other sources, such as magazines and books. The standard answer is that 250 words are a kind of olly olly oxen free, but more than that constitutes plagiarism. And even the 250 words must come with an attribution, giving credit to the source. You can't just tuck someone else's words into the middle of your piece and pretend they're yours. "Borrowed" words should come with quotes for short passages, and indentations for longer sections.

To be safe, though, it's wise to write for permission to use more than a short paragraph, always including an SASE.

On the other hand, when you've interviewed someone specifically for your book, there is no limitation on quoted material. Your publisher assumes that the quoted person gave you his ideas freely, knowing they were intended for publication. With taped interviews, there's no requirement either, that the subject review his words, which are presumed to be accurate.

The above cautions do not apply to *ideas*, however, which can be lifted with impunity as long as the stealing author finds entirely new ways to state what's been said elsewhere. The rule is, words are automatically copyrighted the minute they're written, while ideas are not.

For years, beginning students have come to me with fears about sending manuscripts to publishers and having their work stolen, and they draw little copyright signs on the first page, . . . which, I point out, does no good but does brand them as novices. "You don't have to worry about a publisher stealing your words," I say. "If he does, you'll make a bundle when you take him to court and prove you've got the original manuscript with the original sentences."

I also point out that yes, a publisher might very well find another writer to recast your ideas, but that the writer will have to come up with an entirely different set of words. "In publishing," I say, "it's not what you have to say, but how you say it that counts. The wording is everything."

Inevitably somebody mentions Hollywood.

Ah, Hollywood. Flip the publishing coin and you've got the Movie Business. . . .

When it comes to films, ideas are everything—and exact words mean little or nothing. Producers in Hollywood are forever on the prowl for Great Ideas. Pitch a producer a fantastic idea, and he hardly cares how it's worded. He'll find some seasoned writer to convert the Idea into a Script.

But even that script won't be sacred. The words will be altered and polished and torn apart and re-polished and disposed of and re-invented by everyone within a radius of ten miles—by directors, actors, other script writers, and possibly even the janitor. Nothing is more fluid or less immutable than the words of a Hollywood script.

From everything I've read, including John Gregory Dunne's *Monster*, Hollywood would drive book authors mad; working in the film industry demands forbearance, an air-tight ego, and the patience of a cocker spaniel. To anyone who imagines his words are Golden, Hollywood would be the number one place to avoid.

However, unlike most work in publishing, the money is great.

A FEW FINAL WORDS about writing nonfiction. Standards are constantly rising. While logic, excellent English skills, and the ability to gather and organize new ideas, were once the chief requirements for nonfiction, this is no longer true. Some of today's nonfiction writers are almost as creative and imaginative as their fellow fictionaires. It's no longer enough to state a thought clearly and succinctly. For today's audience you must sometimes be humorous, dramatic, offbeat, at times even startling.

An exercise book called, *Be a Loser*, by Greer Childers, is more than a treatise on yoga-like exercises, it's also a fun and smart-alecky read, as in the following: "So what is it you need to get with the program? Just fifteen minutes a day, first thing in the morning... What should you wear? Your pj's will suffice... You don't have to leave your house, your cat, your refrigerator ..." She even has a section titled, "Why I got off my butt."

With every paragraph Childers writes about exercising, she includes a sentence or two that is pure wisecrack.

Childers, like so many of today's nonfiction writers, has learned that nonfiction readers want more than ideas. They want to be entertained. Amused. Surprised. Delighted. Amazed.

THE MORE I READ, the more I realize that my earlier beliefs about the relatively simple task of writing nonfiction were wrong. I've since discovered it's so challenging and makes such a heavy demand on the right, creative brain (or is it the left?) we writers might as well give in and write fiction.

## Chapter Sixteen

# *AN EAGLE IS DOWN* —
# A FIRST LOOK AT PLOT

AS I STARTED AGAIN on my memoir, I imagined there'd be
a transformation at the typewriter, a wiser me tackling an old job,
instantly able to perceive the problems and intricacies of producing
a salable memoir.

All this for no good reason, of course, but more in the spirit of one
book ended and now it's New Year's Day . . . with all the itchy, pointy
aspects of the prior year behind us and only optimism remaining. I
think I prefer New Year's Day to all others, if only because it makes
the coming year seem so *available*, so *promising*, so *not used up*. Three
hundred and sixty-four days ahead to produce a really terrific memoir
and get it published.

Having successfully completed a non-fiction, I'd forgotten about
all those dropped threads in the memoir, momentarily unaware that I
was now returning to a task with ten times the degree of difficulty.

THIS IS NO EXAGGERATION. The first day of each school year I
always ask the students in my novel-writing class, "How many of you
have been published?" and always a few proud hands go up, usually
from the new people.

"Anybody published in fiction?"

No hands go up. My old students smile because they know what's coming. "Welcome to the best and the worst writing job you can attempt," I say. "On alternate days you'll love it and hate it—and on the worst days you'll feel like ripping up everything you've written." I explain that nothing is harder to create than good fiction, that once you know how it's supposed to read you'll go crazy when your paragraphs come out jerky or murky, or when the story stares at you from your screen and refuses to budge.

On the other hand, euphoria begins when the words start to flow, when little streams become torrents of pure creativity and there you are, with lines that sparkle . . . and half the time you don't know where they came from.  I tell the newcomers we have a rule, that we never critique harshly, that we always look for the good lines and the good paragraphs. On the other hand, we always tell the truth, meaning we note the bad stuff, too.

And then we begin critiquing (tactfully) whatever manuscripts they've brought, and the newcomers can see that their fiction-writing errors are as plentiful as dandelions, and in fact the lawn may soon have to be torn out and replanted. Eventually the newbies perceive what the older students have already grasped: while the process of writing novels is so absorbing that hours and days simply disappear, it's harder than most of us ever dreamed, as daunting as playing the violin; in fact it's a wonder people ever succeed at either one.

I think about violin players all the time. I imagine myself trying to learn, and how impossible it must be, because all up and down the neck of the violin are no guidelines, no definite places to place one's fingers, so you have to do it by *feel*, and then tune your notes by acute listening. . . .

Writing novels is not so different in some ways from playing the violin. The guidelines for memoirs and novels are vague at best, and in the end you succeed mostly by feel, and always by endless, keen listening.

Like violin playing, when you do it right, novel-writing creates a rare state of joy. Better still, you're left with pages in your hands, tangible sheets to keep forever.

Even first drafts can be stimulating. Images appear out of nowhere: red leaves layered on a forest floor, the curved legs of an old piano, stolidly planted in a corner of the room. Characters begin speaking, often better than you do. Some newly-created soul dares to try things you never would.

THOUGH I GRASPED BY the early eighties that Bobby would be the subject of *An Eagle is Down,* (thus the title change), I'd no inkling where to start the book.

That elusive first page again. Why was it so difficult? Why must the weight of the entire book rest on the feeble shoulders of one page?

In my class the subject keeps coming up, and sometimes I find myself going on and on.

But that's only because speakers, teachers, and fellow writers have hammered the subject in my presence, relating horror stories about how editors and agents and their readers, with desks piled to the ceiling, give a newcomer's manuscript one cursory look, five to twenty lines, and that's all . . . how their goal is not manuscript-buying but desk-clearance . . . and how, if a writer isn't wonderful on the first page, a la *Angela's Ashes*, his manuscript will indeed be ashes.

"So all the writing you do after the first page," I say to my class, "is a waste. I mean, if nobody ever reads it, what's the point?" Then I fix them with a hard look. "*No amount of effort is too much to get a wonderful first page.*"

LIKE OTHERS, I DISCOVERED that knowing something does not translate automatically into doing it.

During the struggle with *An Eagle is Down*, I must have started the book with twenty different first pages . . . a few so dramatic I've still got them tucked away because it's so wrenching to throw out a perfectly good first page.

Trouble was, even a great first page wasn't enough; the project needed a wonderful first chapter. It was no use having a fantastic page that didn't lead anywhere. I began to see some of those first pages as false doors on a stage—you open them, and behind the door there's a blank wall, . . . which is when it struck home that while a terrific first page may be necessary, it's far from sufficient.

If my book was going to be about Bobby, his troubled youth had to be included—yet how was I to start the book dramatically while still finding a way to portray Bobby as a boy?

I knew immediately that the book couldn't start with his birth; only for a celebrity like Winston Churchill can you begin with the day he was born. So the search was on for a high, dramatic moment.

A dozen vivid moments were chosen, written, and tossed out: the hang glider crash of a friend; Bobby's eight-hour time-aloft record; his winning the British championships by landing on one foot; the eulogy at his grave site.

None of them worked because, like a path that stops abruptly at a cliff, none were leading anywhere. I could tweak the manuscript all day long, and those incidents refused to take me where I needed to go—back to Bobby's childhood.

Eventually I thought of starting with Eric's death.

And of course that led to the family's most agonizing decision—whether to go on with the hang gliding and the family business, or just close our doors. Suddenly, like a burst of rain from a cloudless sky, a key sentence dropped out: "You can't decide where you ought to go until you look at where you've been."

And that was it. That was where to start.

It "worked" but I didn't like it. I didn't like using Eric's accident as a tool, exploiting the death of a son for my own purposes.

Eventually I decided I could hate it all I liked, but Eric's death was the place to start . . . and my using it didn't imply that I'd ever accepted it, only that it happened and deeply affected all of us. In some ways, the book's beginning gave Eric's death the importance it deserved—a turning point in our lives, after which nothing was ever quite the same.

I was a writer and through me other people could come to know and love Eric and Bobby. And that was absolutely all I should make of what I was doing.

So now I had a subject and a beginning. What more does a memoir writer need? Isn't this the moment when we sit down at the computer and watch the rest of the book fly onto the pages as though it's writing itself?

Well . . . not quite.

There was the little matter of Plot, of how to shape my book so it ebbed and flowed in a novel-like structure. It was Pat Kubis, once more, who gave all of us, a class full of eager novices like me, the lecture that forever changed the way we looked at plot.

I remember she said to our class, "I can give you the foundation for plot in one day. Even children's book writers need this classical plot structure." She turned away from the chalkboard to make her point. "I had an author, once, who wrote dozens of children's books and couldn't sell any of them until she heard this lecture, and then she began selling books, one after the other. It's simple, really. It's called the 'W-diagram.'"

With that, Pat scribbled on the chalk board for ten minutes, laying out a big "W"—which I've blatantly stolen and used myself as a teaching tool for the last twenty-one years. For me, plot had always been the big bugaboo, like mathematics or worse . . . in fact plot seemed so off-putting I could never have written a single fiction book, or my memoir, or taught for more than one day without Pat Kubis's "W Diagram."

(Maybe it didn't really originate with her—but that hardly matters, the point is, it works.)

The big "W" is wonderful because it's simple and it's graphic. It's a big, stark pattern that you can see in your brain as you're writing books and starting to stray down meaningless paths.

After Pat laid out the big W, she also drew underneath it another pattern—a little squiggly design that went up, down, up, down, up, down, like little wavelets in the sea, each wavelet the same size, height, and dimensions as all the others.

As I explain to my students, those up and down wavelets are what we're **not** supposed to do, plot wise, but which almost everyone (including me), does—at first. The wavelets are like this

Episodic Plot

and represent the "Episodic Plot"—disdained words in writing, not unlike "Slice of Life." An episodic plot mirrors real life, and thus fails utterly as drama. As professional actors and writers all know, real life is mainly undramatic and usually verges on boring.

So what nobody wants to read is the Episodic Plot—a little good one day, a little bad the next, a little good, then a little bad, and so on, which gives the reader the sense that the book is going nowhere and she'd better stop yawning and get on the treadmill.

The "W diagram," on the other hand, is a Grand Plan, and once the reader senses the story is moving toward a Dramatic Climax—the iceberg that will sink the *Titanic*—he gets anxious and breathless and so excited he has to keep reading.

Here it is:

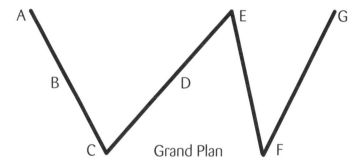

You'll notice it's a skewed "W" with the mid-peak coming toward the end.

Here's how it works. The two outer arms of the "W" represent the start and finish of the protagonist's story. He begins at "A" and is working his way toward "G". The rest of the "W" represents his journey—his path.

At "A", where the story starts, we meet, let's say, Sydney Braveheart, a repressed pharmacist with a new membership in a hiking club and impossible dreams. The tale begins as Sydney pulls a friend aside and confides in an excited whisper that he's planning to climb Mount Everest. The friend, both loyal and decent, averts his eyes from Braveheart's unlikely body and manages not to laugh.

The first leg of the "W", the "A" to "C", represents the barriers to Sydney's goal—all the reasons he'll never do it: he's a novice at climbing, a breathy creampuff of a man who's so out of shape he can barely keep up with his amateur hiking group; he has no money to get to Nepal, let alone buy climbing gear and hire Sherpas; his wife and friends think he's an idiot and would be better off climbing onto a psychiatrist's couch.

But Sydney Braveheart will try. From "C" to "E" he makes plans, overcomes obstacles, and begins doing this crazy thing. He works out daily and takes ever more arduous climbing trips, eventually to places like the Sierras, the Rockies, the Andes, and finally the Himalayas. He attracts sponsors from senior-vitamin and related drug companies (Centrum Silver, Geritol — maybe Viagra) and accumulates enough money to meet his needs. His wife and friends start to admire his whacky courage.

Braveheart's journey from "C" to "E" takes most of the book. The "C" to "E" leg won't be a straight line, or even close. Along his route will be detours, complications, and setbacks, like Sydney's breaking a wrist on Mt. Whitney, his hiring a climbing guide who falls down an escarpment and, worst of all, losing his Viagra sponsorship. But Braveheart is now a fast healer and a tough man, and eventually he reaches the "E" point on our "W diagram."

At "E", Sydney Braveheart, newly-invented tiger of a man, is hunkering down in a tent at base camp, ready to make his final assault on the ferocious mountain. "E" is where our pharmacist's dream, ludicrous as it once seemed, is about to become reality.

But now disaster strikes, the rug pull that takes us from "E" down to "F." (As the reader, you've recognized that Braveheart's life has been going too well for too long. You observe that the book is far from over, and ... Oh boy, oh boy, here comes Trouble.)

And it comes. From "E", plunging to "F", everything that could possibly go wrong, does. A violent blizzard blows up out of nowhere, and Sydney's devoted lead Sherpa, unable to secure the tent, declares the mission over. Sydney Braveheart wakes up with hideous cramps and nausea and can't move. The tent breaks loose and blows away. An oxygen canister rolls down the mountain.

At "F" the climb is over. Nice try, Braveheart, but you'll never make Everest.

Yet somehow, from "F" to "G" our hero fights back. Gutsy man that he is, he persuades his Sherpa to resume the trek, fights back his nausea, and somehow ascends the elusive peak. He reaches "G" on the "W diagram" and plants atop Everest a flag and a pill bottle.

THE "W DIAGRAM" OFFERS the writer a Grand Plan, a classical structure that has been used successfully on stages since the early Greek days. Movies incorporate the structure as well. With its high point coming toward the last third of the story, followed by the great rug pull, the diagram gives the reader a strong sense of the story's overall dramatic layout.

And that's really all there is to it.

There are a number of other plot structures, but if you can make any of the others work, you're already such a gifted novelist you'll be reading this book as an affirmation of your genius.

Additional plot issues are detailed in the next chapter: the pervasive influence of character on plot, thoughts on creativity versus logic, the little plot pest you can't do without—conflict—and where to sleuth out story ideas.

I REMEMBER PAT KUBIS giving us this "W diagram" lecture, and how I looked up from scribbling notes and felt this clutchy feeling in my stomach and realized that little of what she'd said applied to my book. I was thinking, *My story is Real Life and our family events don't fit the "W" shape, or even close, and how am I expected to make it read like a novel?*

I was madly trying to solve the "W" problem, but still having my agent, Patty, send out various inferior versions of *An Eagle is Down.* She said to me one day, "Maralys, since nobody's buying your family story, why don't you try something different? Why don't you write a romance?"

I will always remember my initial reaction: *I can't possibly write a romance, Patty. I've never read one.*

Chapter Seventeen

# MORE ABOUT PLOT

IN STEPHEN KING'S BOOK, *On Writing*, not much was said about plot. In fact the reader gets the impression he adamantly refuses to discuss plot in traditional terms, saying instead, "Plot is, I think, the good writer's last resort and the dullard's first choice. The story which results from it is apt to feel artificial and labored."

While King talks at length about intuition, and a process by which the author "digs up" or unearths a pre-existing story, he pretty much dismisses what most of us think of as formal plotting ... and it goes without saying he'd consider outlines and diagrams the lowest rungs on the plot ladder.

That said, there's probably some cheating going on. Stephen King does instinctively and in his head what most authors have to learn ... that telling a good story requires more than a simple recording of events. There's an issue of progression, of recognizing which events need to be enlarged and played out fully, of grasping the story's outline in its largest sense.

In the prior chapter, I described the "W" diagram and how an overall grand structure is needed to give the reader a sense that the story has momentum and is headed toward some kind of dramatic climax. Think of the "W" diagram as a template, never stifling of creativity, but a way to visualize your story's silhouette.

More limiting would be an outline—chapter-by-chapter, or event-by-event, which some of us need at first like ropes on Everest, to keep us from falling into a crevasse. As I outline my story I'm thinking rapidly and freely, pouring out ideas however they come to me, moving as fast as I can from one event to another. It's brainstorming, never a wasted process.

But a finished outline can't be the holy grail. If, in the actual writing of scenes, the characters begin pulling in another direction, it's okay, cut them loose and forget the outline.

Which brings up a crucial point: **Character is absolutely vital to plot**.

Almost independently, it seems, your characters make story choices; it becomes obvious they will not do certain things, and once you get a feel for them, it's the characters who decide what happens next. From then on your outline is useless.

Here's an example: Atticus Finch, in *To Kill a Mockingbird*, wouldn't mistreat an opponent in a trial any more than he'd lie to his children. It's conceivable that in an early draft, Harper Lee wrote a courtroom scene in which Finch was sarcastic and biting as he interrogated the miscreant, Bob Ewell ... but if so, she surely found herself re-writing, painting Finch as the consummate gentleman, even in this confrontational scene.

It's possible Harper Lee didn't know Atticus quite so well at first. Most of us don't get inside our characters' skins until we've lived with them intimately, which is when the rebellion starts, when the characters rise up and direct the drama.

IN MY OWN EFFORTS to create good plot, I've always felt that nature didn't endow me with great, intuitive flashes of creativity. Instead, I have to get where I'm going by logic.

One day I explained this to my class, only to have one of my best, most creative writers speak up and claim she wasn't given great, intuitive flashes, either.

I said, "You weren't?"

"No. I have to think and think about where the story's going. It doesn't just come to me."

I shook my head. "I thought your great ideas just rained down out of the sky."

She laughed. "I wish."

I explained the "creative process" as it works for me. Since inspiration seldom just "comes," I have to follow a logic trail, asking myself, "What would this character do in this situation?"

In my techno-thriller, *Scatterpath*, for plot purposes I needed to have a woman pilot crash a small plane, and the crash had to be pilot error. So why would a competent woman pilot suddenly become incompetent? Because she was on drugs, perhaps? Legitimate drugs? A pain killer? And why would she be taking a painkiller, and why wouldn't her husband know? Because she'd just had an abortion, perhaps . . . . because of a secret affair, maybe? And why did she have this affair? What kind of person was she? And what kind of man was her husband?

These were not major characters in the book, but still I had to invent logical motivations for what they did, and logical repercussions for what followed . . . that an NTSB investigator who learns unexpectedly that his beloved niece was piloting a downed plane, abruptly loses his objectivity and refuses to believe the crash was pilot error. Instead, an immediate conflict arises with his fellow investigator, who knows the truth but hesitates to put his colleague through the agony of blaming someone he loves.

All logic, every bit. No flashes of intuition at all, just getting where you need to go by a different route. The "What if" route.

I still maintain that certain creative souls receive inspiration from the cosmos. But for the rest of us, logic is a pretty good substitute.

IN THIS DISCUSSION OF plot and creativity, we're missing a key element.

Conflict.

You might call conflict the building block of plot. Without conflict, plot is lifeless. Dull.

For anyone who doubts this, here's an illustration:

Imagine yourself seated on a park bench next to two women

discussing their children. You're faced away from them, disinterested in anything they might say. But let one of the women say, "I'm trying to get our volleyball coach fired. He's been abusing our boys," and right away you're thinking, What did he do? What kind of abuse?

The second woman: "Frankly, I thought he was a nice guy."

First woman: "He's not a nice guy. His personal life is a mess. The kids have seen him doing illegal things behind the bleachers. He's even threatened some of them."

What illegal things? You're thinking. The man takes it out on the kids? What's this all about, anyway?

The second woman: "You have to cut the man some slack. He had a terrible childhood."

"We all had terrible childhoods. But I don't get high and threaten my son."

Without knowing any of the characters, you're suddenly interested in their lives, eavesdropping on their mini-drama because conflict is so inherently interesting. It raises so many story questions. Who? Why? How? When?

Conflict is like a crash beside the highway. Here are all these people you've never met, but just put them in a perilous situation with police lights flashing and cars mangled and they, the victims, sprawled about, and all at once you're burning to know everything about them. Who are they? What caused the accident? What's to become of them?

Conflict is your story's attention-grabber, your tale's accident by the side of the road. Conflict is always exciting, always insistent.

I tell my students that conflict wears all kinds of faces, few of them violent. It doesn't mean people are pummeling each other, only that they're disagreeing. Conflict can be as subtle as a sharp look, a small, digging comment, or a tightening of the lips . . . or as overt as a man holding a gun.

Conflict can be a sailor in a small boat battling tumultuous seas; it can be a woman facing down cancer; it can be a prisoner fighting to prove his innocence; it can be a young skier buried under an avalanche.

Conflict can be expressed humorously, in the tart come-back. Or in sarcasm.

Conflict is essential to drama. So essential, in fact, that it's needed in almost every scene. When a student turns in a chapter in which everyone agrees with everyone else and nobody is faced with a real problem and nary a harsh word is spoken, I have to remind the student gently that it reads too much like real life. Everyday life is, after all, just everyday life . . . and most of it rocks along without conflict—and is therefore unexciting.

A scene without conflict is acceptable only when it serves as a breather, or a wrap-up after earlier, highly-dramatic or extremely tense scenes. Occasionally, in the midst of mind-spinning drama, the writer needs to slow the pace, giving the reader a brief pause to take a calming breath.

As we wrap up a class discussion on conflict, I say to my students, "You have to keep asking yourself the same question as you write each scene: Where's the conflict? After awhile, finding and weaving in conflict becomes second nature."

IN SOME WAYS *ALL novels are mysteries.* I say this in class often. All good novels contain suspense, unanswered questions, uncertain outcomes. Not all tales are *murder mysteries,* but all stories must keep the reader anxious and wondering. Savvy authors withhold enough information so there's always a story question hanging out in space. Even as one question is answered, another is raised, so the reader can never relax.

Now here's a major plotting issue: how much information should be given to the protagonist? Should our hero know everything the reader knows . . . should he be aware that the bad guys are planting bombs all around his house . . . or do we keep him ignorant until the last chapter?

Some authors prefer to let the protagonist in on the nasty secrets as they develop, so the reader learns each new story twist at the same moment the hero learns it, and feels all the shifting emotions along with the protagonist.

Other writers prefer to keep the reader informed, but not the protagonist. They want us to be afraid, nervous, and worried, even though the protagonist may be calm as butter.

Some authors let the story play out without keeping anyone apprised of the secrets, waiting until the last few pages to "wrap up" the entire plot. I've always found this construction unsatisfying and feel I've missed most of the drama. No matter how clever the wrap-up, the reader can hardly grasp or fully appreciate a tangled web of plot twists which are all dumped on him in one great load at the end.

As a teacher and reader, I'm an advocate of "tell 'em everything." To me, tense stories are far more gripping when the protagonist is kept in the loop and on edge . . . when he is made to suffer page by page along with the reader. I want to see each rotten deed, feel each disaster through the hero's eyes. I want to see him spinning in the wind. And I will always care more if *he* cares.

It's hard to imagine John Grisham's *The Firm* being half as exciting without the main character, Mitch, experiencing each new event as a slowly-growing continuum of horror. Of course, we readers knew a few things Mitch didn't know, at least not at first, but that's okay, it's just a shade of gray.

No DISCUSSION OF PLOT would be complete without addressing that oft-asked question, "Where do you get your ideas?"

Beginning writers can't conceive that to a seasoned author, ideas are everywhere, behind every raised eyebrow, behind every closed door. The longer you write, the more story ideas you see in everyday life: story ideas are found on the evening news, in newspapers, in overheard snatches of conversation, in relationships between people you know (or people you've heard of), sometimes in simple wanderings of the mind. *What if. . .* ?

Last week in our town, a respected high school teacher (a Teacher of the Year), abruptly disappeared. His wife cried on the evening news, claiming he would never desert her or their tiny baby. His last known act was removing a small amount of money from an ATM; everyone speculated about foul play and the media implied he'd soon be found dead.

After four mysterious days, and new rumors that the man had had a fight with his wife before he disappeared, the teacher was found registered in a Las Vegas hotel.

The story unfolded over days. A last item in our local newspaper stated that the man was "sick," and had returned to his mother's town.

A small story, but full of fascinating questions: Why did the man leave so abruptly? Why didn't he tell his wife? Was anyone else involved? Why only a small amount of money from the ATM? How sick was sick? In the hands of a talented writer, this germ of an idea could form the heart of a novel—expanded in all directions, of course.

But such are the small ideas that beckon to writers from everywhere . . . most of which never become novels, but a few of which do.

For some writers, a novel begins forming around a vivid character. For others, a novel springs from the twisting of a cliché. Elegant writer Elizabeth George did this when she pitted an esteemed lady prime minister against the editor of a sleazy newspaper. Her twist was magnificent. The PM became the true sleaze and the editor the character with guts and integrity.

For more of us, I'd guess, a novel grows from an intriguing event, an odd situation, or a "What if?" question. What if airplanes began crashing, for instance, and nobody, including the NTSB, could figure out why—or even what, exactly, was going wrong? Such was the question I asked as I began my techno-thriller, *Scatterpath*.

NEWCOMERS ASK AS WELL, "Don't you ever run out of ideas?" The answer is No.

For all of us who see drama on all sides, in every corner of our worlds, it's not ideas we run out of, but time. There's never enough time to turn every intriguing idea we come across into a full-blown story. Which is why so many of us keep folders with book ideas tucked away, lest the well inexplicably runs dry.

But it never does. The more ideas you use, the more you seem to find. Once you label yourself "novelist," your subconscious begins its search, and ideas keep presenting themselves, and the only caution I can offer here is that you've got to find a piece of paper, quick, and write them down. Because you really will hate yourself when you're thinking a few days later, Now what was that great story idea I had in the grocery store?

AS A NOVELIST, I am often approached by people who feel they've led fascinating lives and are looking for someone to write their memoirs. Regretfully, I turn them down—not because I'm afraid the story won't be any good, but only because of my own backlog of projects. Which seems to be the case with most novelists. We're just too busy to take on someone else's exciting story.

IN THE END, GOOD plot does not have to be wickedly complicated (though many are). The essence of great plot derives from that subtle ability known as good story-telling. And I swear, you either have it or you don't. I can name a few best-selling authors (but I won't), who make all kinds of writing errors that drive me crazy, but are such good story tellers they're published anyway. And readers go on loving them.

AFTER ALL THIS TALK about plot, I honestly believe that if you love to tell stories, if you keep the "W" diagram in focus, if you create vital, believable characters, and if you fill your scenes with conflict, you probably already have a good plot.

Chapter Eighteen

# WRITING ROMANCES FOR THE LOVE OF IT

THE "W DIAGRAM" ARRIVED in my writing life at an opportune moment, just as I'd decided to take my agent's advice and consider writing a romance. With only faint regret, I looked back over my shoulder at *An Eagle Is Down,* sitting abandoned in its box near my desk, a loose pile of pages that signified little except blind hope. It was like leaving an unproductive farm and moving to town and getting a job in a soda fountain. I was tired of working the soil, tired of nothing coming up. I could dispense sodas for awhile and see if something else might happen.

Even so, I wasn't exactly sure, at first, that I wanted to write a romance. Having never read any, my sense of their contents came from the half-naked women whose bosoms protruded beyond the covers and into the aisles of our grocery store. You practically had to detour around them. I'd always regarded them as not-quite-books.

Still, Patty had said, "You may not know this, Maralys, but romances are selling like crazy," and suddenly I was thinking, *You've aroused my competitive spirit.* (Which her husband said all the time.) Thrilled by the words "selling like crazy," I bought six romances and read them.

They were terrible.

Four out of six were so bad it seemed astonishing that publishers had ever taken them seriously—much less paid to print them. *What were the editors thinking?*

I might not have known much, but I recognized wimpy writing when I saw it. The four bad ones were so *stilted.* So awkward and self-conscious. So mushy. So full of things like, "she said nastily," "he said jokingly," "she asked painfully," "he said clumsily," "she squeaked," "he barked," "she hissed," "she mewed," and people running around behind themselves explaining everything they said, including the things they said nastily or jokingly.

One of the six was marginal. And one was quite good, meaning it read like any other book.

I called up Patty. "I'll try it," I said.

To myself I was thinking, *I can certainly beat out the bad four.*

So there I was, about to jump ship once more, genre-hopping like a fool.

EVEN WITH THE "W diagram" at the ready, ideas for a romance did not come springing out to greet me. In fact, no ideas appeared at all. I wondered if this was a simpleton's journey, setting off to write a book without the slightest inkling of what should be in it. Faced with the need to create a wholly made-up story, something I'd never tried before, I was frankly at a loss. How did romance writers begin, anyway? From what reservoir of untapped conflicts and untried situations did they get their ideas?

It couldn't be this hard for everyone; surely some writers simply *start.*

Aware once more that I was short on creativity, I began casting about for a writing partner, someone with **Ideas.**

That's when I thought of my daughter-in-law, Betty-Jo. Who was more of a reader than she? I could still see her out on the hill where Chris was flying hang gliders, sitting on a rock with a book in her lap, able to jet through a novel in half the time it took anyone else.

Aware that she had more than enough going on her in life, with two small daughters and a husband working 24-hour shifts as an orthopedic resident, I approached her gingerly. "Betty-Jo, how would you like to collaborate on a romance?"

Even as she paused to think, I remembered another significant plus, her master's degree in library science.

She didn't hesitate long. "Maybe I can," she said. "As long as I don't have to do the actual writing."

*Great*, I thought. *Wonderful.*

She asked, "How do you picture us going about it?"

"Well. I was hoping you could dream up a plot, because that's where I'm deficient. I've got a decent right brain but apparently no left brain." *See how lopsided I walk?* "If you can feed me a plot, I can probably write the book."

She smiled. "I'll try. But I haven't read many romances. Practically none. I guess I should buy some."

"Take mine," I said, and decided not to forewarn her. "They'll give you an idea of our competition."

A week later, Betty-Jo said, "I see why you thought we could do this."

We agreed to split the money fifty-fifty which, if anybody gave us any, would be especially nice for her, because at the moment Chris earned practically nothing.

In no time, with our two heads together and a lot of stimulation flying between houses, we decided to set our story on a romantic resort in the Virgin Islands . . . a classic example of writing what you know, because the four of us had vacationed at Caneel Bay during Chris's first traumatic year of medical school.

A WEEK LATER, BETTY-JO brought me a dozen scrawled pages on lined paper, written in her inscrutable handwriting. She, who is one of the smartest and most balanced people I know, has the handwriting of a schizophrenic.

"I'll have to read it to you, I guess," she said, and after we plopped her baby in a playpen, we pulled our chairs close to my typewriter and went to work.

WRITING THE BOOK WAS fun.

Actually, doing anything with Betty-Jo is fun—which must be one of the reasons Chris decided so early, while they were both still in high school, that he would marry her.

For months we talked back and forth, argued without rancor, and wrote like mad. We were on the phone every day, defending our positions where they diverged, hammering out details. Betty-Jo wouldn't tolerate any loose threads: no silly encounters between our lovers, no unmotivated tantrums, not one line of corny dialogue. "But he wouldn't *do that,* Maralys, he'd never just show up in the middle of the night to be irritating. And she wouldn't snap at him like a shrew, either."

"We're short on conflict, you know."

"If we are, we'll fix it, but they've got to argue about something important. Our characters aren't a couple of ninnys."

With Betty-Jo, I was always defending myself. *Thinking. Then re-thinking.*

I began to see she was unrelenting in her analyses, as pleasantly stubborn, even German, as I was. I may have been the ship's captain, but she was the navigator, and if she didn't actually hold the wheel, she had her eye on the compass. I could easily have steered the ship onto every sand bar in the river. But not with her along.

Together, we created our heroine and hero out of spunky people we both knew, dreamed up lively scenes which grew wilder the more we talked, invented raging conflicts, wrote sex scenes, and laughed at our inventions.

Laughter. That's what I remember best—the fun, at times verging on hilarity. We knew the sex romps were absurd and at times over-explicit, but that's what editors wanted. So we gave it to them.

We'd planned to write a "short" romance, about 60,000 words, but somewhere mid-creation Patty happened to say casually, "The long romances seem to be selling right now, better than the short ones. And they're making more money," and just as casually Betty-Jo and I said to each other, "Oops. Let's go for a long one," and we flipped a little switch in our brains and wrote on.

It was all so arbitrary. So light-hearted. So not like real work.

Five months after we began, we sent Patty a 100,000 word manuscript. Surprised, but not too surprised, we learned she liked it.

The next step went far beyond surprise. In only about three weeks

Patty sold our book. For $10,000.

That night Chris and Betty-Jo and Rob and I went out to celebrate . . . dinner for the two wives who'd earned a fast $10,000.

A week later came the ultimate surprise: Harlequin Superromances had calculated our word count with a mysterious, home-grown system that was so hard to fathom Betty-Jo and I had simply ignored it and figured out the word total another way. Now the editors told us the manuscript was 5,600 words too long, meaning we had to cut twenty-five pages.

"Twenty-five pages!" we moaned, agreeing that this would ruin the book, that our perfect story couldn't survive a twenty-five page cut.

Actually, it could. Trimming and cutting became a challenge, even fun, like solving a puzzle. And the book grew steadily better. "This word can go." "What does that line add, anyway?" "Hey, here's a whole scene, I always thought it was kind of dumb, let's just dump it."

When Harlequin told us later they'd misfigured (we could have told them their system was no good), and now we had to put some of our cuts back, we argued that we'd made the book tighter and couldn't we just leave it alone, and they said we could.

With the changes sent off, Betty-Jo said, "It's time we came up with a new title."

In a single non-thinking minute, we'd arbitrarily assigned *Tempest and Tenderness,* to our manuscript, simply to give it a handle. We considered it a throw-together, nothing you could take seriously.

To our surprise—our horror—the editors of Harlequin Superromances wanted to keep it. They were adamant; they wanted the book exactly as we'd titled it.

"Can you believe this?" I said. "Next time we'll have to be more careful. Lord . . . *Tempest and Tenderness.* They have to be kidding."

Rob said, "You going to let them keep that disgusting title?"

I stared at him; suddenly the title didn't seem so bad. "Sorry we didn't ask you first. But now we're stuck. They won't budge."

"Romances . . ." he said.

"Ten thousand dollars," I said. "It's a story. And not a bad one, either. So pipe down about romances."

SOON I WAS REGULARLY attending romance writers' meetings, the RWA (Romance Writers of America), talking to other writers, learning from my own experience and others' that the craft was not as "easy" as everyone thought . . . nor an art form that deserved to be demeaned or denigrated. I could see that writing is writing, and if you do it well enough, it can evolve into worthwhile leisure reading, romance or not. I was pleased with our first effort.

I also observed that romance writers were getting better, striving to improve their techniques and make the books more mainstream. The corny tags, "He sneered," "she whimpered," were disappearing.

In addition, editors were beginning to look for themes that went beyond the narrow confines of "him-her," "him-her." They were willing to accept tough, controversial issues, like rape, abortion, politics, physical handicaps, racism, divorce, as long as they were done tastefully. So you could now touch on rape, as long as you made it somehow . . . tasteful.

About then I was elected president of our local RWA, and the next time Rob said, "Oh . . . romances," I told him to stuff it. Forever.

ONE DAY PAT KUBIS offered me a gift I'd long coveted: a teaching job. One of her classes at Orange Coast College had overflowed, and she asked if I wanted to take the romance writers, and I said, "You're kidding! How did you know I've always dreamed of being a writing teacher?"

"I *didn't* know. I just guessed you could do it."

So there I was, scrounging through drawers for my old elementary school teaching credential, then applying for a community college credential . . . and getting it! Which was, to my surprise, a lifetime credential.

In 1984 began a long period of Wonderful Wednesdays. One night a week, for many years, I've disappeared into a kind of teachers' Garden of Eden, where people come because they want to. Where students arrive with manuscripts in tow, hoping to pick up useful tidbits, where they scoop up every scrap of writing insight I can offer. Where authors strive and improve and sometimes create magic . . . where writers are anxious to absorb all the big and little discoveries that I, and they, keep making about the craft.

All this time I've known we were all in it together. Day after day, we're all still learning.

OVER THE NEXT FEW years Betty-Jo and I sold three more long romances, always striving for improvement, hopeful that our books were getting more passionate and at the same time more believable.

"Passionate" was always tricky. What were the editors thinking, anyway—soft porn or hard porn? How much detail did they want?

More important, how much detail did *we want*? How much blushing, how much squirming?

After awhile we learned tricks, which will be covered in the next chapter—stratagems for being specific without verging on raw.

From time to time, I brought little homilies to our writing sessions, rules-of-thumb I'd picked up from other writers. "I've just learned the definition of a conflict," I said to Betty-Jo one day. "In the poorly-written books you've got this heroine, say Cynthia, who doesn't *know* her lover is really the King of Sweden. Somehow he never thinks to tell her, but if they'd talked for five minutes she'd *find out* why his calls come in over a secure telephone, and why he has to keep rushing off to Scandinavia to do kingly things, and why she can never reach him in America. This is not a conflict—it's a misunderstanding."

Betty-Jo said, "I've always hated books like that."

"Me too," I said. "But true conflict is different. The hero can argue all day long that it's good for everyone when skiers use a mountain and enjoy it up close. And the heroine can argue just as vehemently that skiers destroy the wilderness and a mountain needs to be kept unscarred and pristine. *That's* a real conflict, because one conversation won't make it go away."

Such was the ecology conflict that became the core of our second book, *Mountain Spell* . . . another terrible title, except this time the editors chose it over Rob's more eloquent, *My Man, My Mountain*, and nothing Betty-Jo or I could say would dissuade them.

In this, our second book, with the words carefully counted using Harlequin's weird, unreliable system, our book turned out 25 pages too short! So there we were again, once more adjusting the core of our story to fit a counting system that deserved to be discarded like a faulty calculator.

FOR A FEW YEARS Betty-Jo and I continued our partnership, basing each new book on one of my personal experiences, so that I, with my empty left brain, would have something concrete to write about. After we'd finished with the conflict about Mount Shasta, where I grew up, we wrote a romance based on my other love, tennis, and this time they kept our title, *A Match for Always*.

Betty-Jo never cared what subject we chose; both sides of her brain performed equally.

Though we tried to woo editors with our fourth book, whose core issue was hang gliding, they kept turning us down. Within a few years we'd sent in three, hundred-page proposals—enough prose for a whole novel. But we kept getting rejected, and for the oddest of reasons: we knew too much. Our enthusiasm for hang gliding's beauty, our knowledge of details, and our unwillingness to skim lightly over the topic, tended to drown out the romance.

Yet when we finally sold it, *Soar and Surrender* became our finest book—the most believable conflict, the most realistic characters, and yes . . . our best feel for the topic. By then I'd somehow fired up my left brain, trained it or teased it or hammered it into submission, until I was finally plotting on par with Betty-Jo.

Among the lessons we learned was How to Write Love Scenes.

Chapter Nineteen

# WRITING LOVE SCENES

THE DEEPER I GOT into writing category romances, the clearer it became that men and women view them differently. I mean **really differently.**

The women who read traditional romances love them unconditionally, the way you love your child, and read them in bunches, maybe a dozen a week.

Not so with men, who don't read romances at all. On that subject men tend to be neutral, with scant interest and the dimmest of attitudes.

But wait. That's not quite true. A few men do have attitudes. You mention you're writing a romance and a tiny minority grin salaciously and make offhanded, sniggering comments and it's obvious what they're thinking. The quips can be veiled but the attitude is clear: a romance novel is a sex novel. It's about "the act," and just "the act," because why else would women write them? If an author mentions love, these fellows look surprised. More than once I've seen a man grab one of my romance novels and begin searching for "those scenes," grinning slyly to himself like a miner who imagines he's about to find the world's richest gold nugget.

I just let them look. *If you find one*, I'm thinking, *you'll be disappointed.*

It's the covers, of course, that scream lewd and lascivious, that taint the genre and bring on the smirks. A number of romance novelists, including me, disparage the bawdiest and crudest among them. Stereotyped as they are, the nudie-booby lust jackets suggest to the uninitiated that the contents must be nothing more than one long romp between the sheets.

And indeed, that's sometimes true.

But most of the time it isn't. Romance novels are exactly what the name says . . . relationship stories about romance. About love. About tenderness. About caring. And yes, about passion. But first and foremost, they're about love.

These stories are fulfillment fantasies, bringing women temporary respite from a world where they may not feel loved half enough. Within these covers an ordinary woman turns beautiful and finds her ideal soul-mate, the near-perfect man who may not "get it" at first, but eventually figures out and grasps what a woman yearns for most. This is the man who brings a woman the unconditional love she's craved all her life. And this larger-than-life hero might even throw in some conversation.

I've heard women say, "Men ought to read romance novels. If they really want to understand love from a woman's viewpoint, they'd study them. Our attitudes are all there, written large and clear. We want men to love us. We want them to talk to us."

OF COURSE THE STORIES are sexy, too, and passion does have a way of culminating the way the slyest guys think it does . . . but only as the ultimate expression of sublime, enduring love. And always with the hero's passion confined to one—and only one—woman.

Nowhere in these books do men express their love the way they do in real life—by fixing the leak under the bathroom sink.

So there you have it. Vive la difference!

SINCE MEN ARE NOT expected to read these books, and don't, the sex scenes are usually written from a woman's viewpoint. Some are blatant, almost pornographic, called by one friend, "the loin achers."

Others are not so explicit.

Over the years, the standards for love scenes have changed. In the earliest days of romance novels, written by love goddesses like Barbara Cartland in England, love scenes ended at the bedroom door. Kisses were the ultimate in physical expression; the rest you simply had to imagine.

Even in the early '80s, when Betty-Jo and I began writing romances, a few romance lines still clung to the old traditions, called themselves "sweet" romances, and eschewed all sex scenes, graphic or otherwise.

The books in the big middle group that the two of us wrote for included love scenes of varying degrees of explicitness and intensity—and lots of funny euphemisms like "his throbbing member."

On the outer fringes were the lines known as "steamy," with sweaty, heavy-breathing, rhythmic, palpitating scenes that went on for pages.

Back then, Harlequin and Silhouette's middle-group gave their authors some leeway. The editors wanted sex, but the authors were in charge of the Hays office and could set their own decency standards—and we did. Whatever Betty-Jo and I really hated to read about, like tongues crawling around in other people's mouths, we left out. We never referred to the male anatomy, throbbing or otherwise, and we kept the actual him-into-her vague and non-specific.

We had a problem, of course. The scenes had to be long enough to satisfy editors, and just specific enough so readers knew what was going on. But we didn't see the need to describe all the anatomical parts (except breasts, which had always been fair game), in damp, pulsing detail.

Even the editors themselves seemed conflicted about love scenes. Important editors came to our RWA meetings and told us that readers admitted skipping over the bedroom scenes because they were all alike and slowed down the action . . . but on the other hand, sexy books inexplicably sold better than non-sexy.

All of us, editors and writers alike, were groping in the dark, feeling our way along slippery passageways.

Fortunately, partly thanks to Colleen McCullough's *Thornbirds*, Betty-Jo and I found a great example of how to do what we wanted and still satisfy everyone. Drawing on the scene where Meggie finally makes love to her priest, we saw that sex *in the realm of imagination, mind, spirit, and feelings* can make pretty intense reading after all. Never does McCullough, in this scene, sink to describing body parts, though the reader knows exactly what's happening. Here, the author elevates sex to a purer form, in the realm of spirituality and sublimity, so that feelings—make that love—rather than physical sensations predominate. Yet I swear, this is one of the sexiest sex scenes I've ever read. Colleen McCullough's approach inspired us to aim for similar, elevating effects.

We found we could expand our love scenes by making setting one of the ingredients: the perfume of flowers, the wafting of warm air, the light pouring into a room and illuminating a face or a crown of rich, auburn hair. We used wild, windy storms; heavy rain beating on the roof; the howling of winds.

We discovered that a lengthy lead-in, plus the hero and heroine's breathless awareness of each other's fine qualities, worked to enrich our scenes. We tried to lean heavier on things like eyes, hands, facial expressions, personality, tone of voice . . . while paying less attention to the purely sexual aspects of our lovers' bodies.

We lingered in areas of the mind, concentrated on feelings and desires . . . reserving for last a few brief, but not-too-explicit, paragraphs on the sexual act itself.

HERE ARE EXCERPTS FROM the first love scene in our category romance, *Soar and Surrender*. The hero, Kirk, is a rigid, by-the-rules, commercial airline pilot, and Jenny an unpredictable free spirit. In this scene the two are beginning to discover that the stereotypical images they've held of each other aren't necessarily true. Kirk, usually impatient and not given to altruism, has just urged Jenny to call a far-away uncle who needs their help. The call is successful, and Jenny sees a new side of Kirk.

AFTERWARD SHE AND KIRK sat on his living room couch close together. They'd accomplished something, she thought, a lot, actually. If Kirk hadn't urged her, she'd never have made the call. She just hadn't thought good results were possible. She snuggled closer and said, "Thank you, Kirk."

"For what?"

"For wanting to solve my problems. For caring. For . . . for wanting to make me happy."

"It was the right thing to do, Jenny." He raised her face to his and she saw the hunger in his deep blue eyes and his strong features, not the most handsome man she'd ever met, but the only man she'd ever wanted as much as she wanted him now. She smiled at him impishly. "Along with a kitchen, your house has a bedroom?"

"I seem to remember one somewhere."

"Show it to me," she murmured, pulling his arms up around her neck.

JENNY WEIGHED SO LITTLE Kirk lifted her off the couch effortlessly and carried her in his arms to his bed.

He moved as in a dream, hardly believing she wanted him enough to say so, that the blithe spirit he'd only imagined himself making love to for so long had finally come to him eagerly and without persuasion.

Gently Kirk laid her on his bed . . . almost afraid to acknowledge there was anything out of the ordinary in her being here. Something might happen to make it all change; no one had ever inspired in him such tenderness and longing.

Was it, he thought in a fleeting moment, that she'd always seemed unattainable? A will-o-the-wisp who danced tantalizingly just out of reach?

Perhaps. . . .

Her eyes! She was watching him languidly and he thought, suddenly, how her eyes were the very essence of her, the way he thought of her when he visualized her—warm and liquid and sometimes devilish or inscrutable but always full of promise. He made himself move slowly, willing these moments to last lest they never come again.

JENNY CLOSED HER EYES as Kirk began to undo her blouse. His hands were large and capable, with unexpected gentleness that made her shiver with delight. As he put aside her blouse . . . she let her eyes drift open and noticed, dreamily, how easily he coped with button and hook, how sure and deft all his movements.

She might have known . . . she'd never seen Kirk do anything badly; he was always sure, invariably smooth. But now she relived her feelings of the last two days and felt as if a different man were making love to her—a man who was so much more than she'd thought at first that his dimensions now seemed as unexpected and varied as the weather.

Controlled, well-ordered Kirk. But he hadn't been controlled, not lately, not in the supply room, not now. Where had that man gone? Or hadn't she ever known him very well? . . .

After a while he rose on an elbow and looked down at her, and she opened her eyes. Above her she saw a face she'd once thought she'd known so well she could recite all its moods: coldness, irony, warmth, delight, anger, amusement. But yesterday for a short while there'd been more, a lightheartedness, a relishing of adventure so unlike him she'd wondered if that was something new or merely something long buried.

Now there was more again. Kirk was looking at her with such intensity her yearning for him increased tenfold. In his deeply blue eyes a melting, unexpressed longing seemed to sweep her into his very soul.

"Jenny . . . my Jenny."

BETTY-JO AND I BELIEVED we had to **feel** the emotions, and feel them we did. Without our dedication to living through each scene on an emotional level, we knew we'd never be convincing.

*Thornbirds* is far from being the only book that served as a unique example. *Roses in Winter* by Joan Dial—and many other books— also contain love scenes that seem to float and shimmer above the physical act.

TO SAY THAT THE author's feelings must be included is an understatement. I knew one author who hated to write sex scenes and freely told us so, yet wrote them anyway, in great detail. Unfortunately, her negative feelings crept in and gave her scenes less emotion than a marble figure carved in a Roman bath house . . . a collection of graphic-but-empty words that felt as cold as stone. Yet that same author loved to do research on exotic settings, like India and Turkey, and her love for atmosphere so permeated her books that readers like me fell in love with whatever place she chose to visit.

I tell my students often that their personal feelings will seep into their work, whether they want them to or not. On paper, you just can't hide what you really think.

AN INTERESTING NOTE ON *The Thornbirds.* McCullough chose to write an earlier sex scene between Meggie and her husband, whom she despised, and in this scene, with disgust and avoidance part of the package, the author included every bodily function and managed to make the whole affair seem pure barnyard.

OVER THE YEARS I'VE found, to my surprise, that a few male friends are greater prudes about sex on the written page than women, that they prefer to skip it altogether.

I've also noticed that the more prurient men's books think in terms of conquest of many women, instead of what they consider a hog-tied-and-suffocating relationship to just one.

You might say each of these viewpoints represents a different aspect of nature in the wild. The multi-conquest books are the untamed stallions who guard and service a whole herd of mares. And the category romances represent the swans who mate for life.

EVENTUALLY BETTY-JO AND I relinquished that special era in our lives because, as I told later audiences, "I was running out of personal experiences."

Well, that was partly true. And partly wasn't. By then Betty-Jo had four children, three girls and a boy, and was now twice as busy. And I was growing tired of the limitations imposed by romance. I no longer wanted to concentrate on him-her, him-her, while downplaying everything else. I wanted to move on.

But mainly, I yearned to get back to my first love, my memoir, neglected now for six years. It felt like I'd strayed long enough.

How could I know that three or four more genre-hops were still to come?

Chapter Twenty

# *DOWNWIND*

OFTEN WHEN I READ Rob my latest chapter, he fixes me with a hard stare. "It's perfect, Babe. Perfect! Don't change a word!" Underneath, there's an implied, "You promise?"

I don't promise. I don't say anything. Because later I know I'll look at the piece again, just a quick peek, mind you, a confirming look, and I'll find something that seems to stick out, a line or word I can't live with, that I know in my soul can be made better. And once again I'll start tinkering, and all the time I'll be thinking, Oh, boy, if Rob only knew what I'm doing. . . .

And so it was with *An Eagle is Down* which, if it was truly a perfect book, would have sold in the first year. But it didn't sell and obviously wasn't perfect, so there I was, re-writing it once more.

A NEW DRAFT MEANT it was time to re-name the book.

Re-naming became a rule in my writing life: you re-write a book from scratch, you give it a new title. The reasons aren't all perfectly logical; sometimes you just get tired of the old name. Yet logic figures in too. Often the name no longer fits. The various versions of a book tend to hang around your desk looking like twins, and it's all too easy to pick one up and find you're working on the evil twin. You can't make that mistake once you've changed the running head.

Thus, *An Eagle Is Down* became *Downwind*—which is when I began losing Rob's enthusiasm for my endless project. My husband, so naturally precise he rarely had to write more than a single draft of any legal document, had no patience for doing anything more than once (let alone fifteen times), an attitude reflected in his oft-repeated statement, "Why don't you just *finish* the damned thing?"

I'd feel my face hardening and hear my voice turning defensive. "I thought it was finished, Rob. Each time I wrote it all the way through I thought, That's it, the book is done."

"It'll **never** be finished."

"Of course it will. That's a wild statement and you know it. Wait and see."

An irritated growl combines with a look of disgust. If I had to define my husband's attitude, it would be that he absolutely cannot abide the writing process. Not the way I do it. He can't accept the thought that a sentence we both think is good might still be tinkered with, might still need adjustment. He can't endure watching the book-writing game as it's played in my study—two steps forward and later three steps back. He can't stand knowing that I'm forever starting over and never quite at the finish line. He doesn't accept the fact that I love re-writing—better even than writing. He wants me to run the damned race and get it over with. What kind of business is this, anyway, where a piece of work is never, absolutely never, finished?

I'm sure he thinks I alone am turtle-slow, that nobody else goes through this.

He's wrong. As fellow writers have all urged, my next chapter is entirely devoted to re-writing.

I BEGAN MY LATEST journey with *Downwind*. By then I knew something about plot and how the story should be laid out. Though I puzzled long and hard about "integrity," and "telling the truth," I eventually made an executive decision: if real life doesn't exactly fit the "W diagram," maybe you can **make** it fit.

Okay, you can't cheat. But you can fudge a little. And fudging becomes necessary if your memoir is ever to read like a novel. Which it must. What I did was rearrange events to fit the classical plot structure, so that later I could say in all honesty, "Everything I said happened, actually happened. But it happened in a somewhat different time frame."

Certain months in our hang gliding era were basically dull, so those were telescoped down to a few paragraphs. True to the episodic pattern that defines real life, we as a family experienced a little good one day and a little bad the next, in an endless pattern.

But that wouldn't do for a memoir. After Eric was killed, I grouped within a few chapters all the bad things that had happened to us over a period of years. Eric's death was followed by Bobby's girl friend suffering a serious crash … by our losing the Twentieth Century Fox movie to stunt men … by the betrayal of a trusted hang glider dealer who lied and cheated and stole our customers. With negative grouping, I was able to create a mood that befitted the bottom of the "W diagram," a period of despondency that said the rug had been pulled out from under us and life would never be good again.

It worked.

All the re-arranging of real-life events contributed to a dramatic structure that resembled most well-plotted novels. From beginning to late middle, readers could sense that the story was building, ever building toward a climax … and then they felt that niggling, pit-of-the-stomach sensation that disaster lurked in the shadows.

Then came the disasters themselves.

Luckily, a few triumphs still remained after the rug pull, triumphs my characters had to work for and *earn*. And while the book ended as a tragedy for Bobby, life still held hope for his brother, Chris.

HAVING RESOLVED THE PROBLEMS of focus, first page, initial event, and overall plot, I was left with decisions that should have been easy and weren't, such as who would tell the story—a non-issue for most memoir writers.

My story was unique. A substantial portion was intended to sweep the reader into the hang gliding experience, from early, laughable attempts to fly, to the ultimate adventure—soaring like an eagle. Yet who was I, a mother, to make that seem realistic?

Maybe the book should be written from Chris's viewpoint.

On the other hand, great portions were about Bobby, the stubbornest son who ever existed, and how we, his parents, struggled unsuccessfully to turn him into a conventional person, and how, in the end, Bobby "won" and became exactly the man he'd always envisioned.

How could a brother be expected to understand all that?

With no guidelines, no one coaching from the wings, I wrote the book entirely from Chris's viewpoint. Then I did it again from mine. With each version I left vital insights behind, until a fellow writer finally said, "Why don't you write it from two first-person viewpoints?"

That had never seemed remotely possible. How crazy did I want this project to be? It was already a non-selling manuscript, why would I consider dooming it for sure?

In the end, that's exactly what I did.

And it worked. Or at least it worked after an editor was kind enough to offer a brief critique: "The Chris character has an 'Oh golly, gee-whiz' tone to him." Stopped short by his criticism and not knowing what else to do, I submitted that portion to Chris.

Chris soon called me. "You had a lot of stuff wrong, Mom. It needs tons of work." He paused and continued on a note of disgust that said I'd made the ultimate blunder. "You made me sound like *Erma Bombeck*!"

Oh. Well okay, I said, fix it, and he said he would.

Back again, the material presented a new dilemma. For the sake of honesty, I wanted to use everything Chris had written, but it wasn't possible. His rewrite was so wordy and stilted he came off sounding like a professor of astrophysics—meaning the tone was as badly skewed as before, but this time in the other direction.

In the end, I had to find a balance between his way and my way and somehow make Chris sound like what he'd been all along—a youthful, exuberant male.

EVERYONE WHO WRITES HIS own story knows from the start what will be in the book, or at least he knows the major events. The important, dramatic moments in life are obvious, and all of us who set out to write such a story are sure in part where we're headed.

The problem is the small things. Mainly, everything else.

Is this little incident important, you ask yourself, will anyone care about Bobby's lesser flights, will they care that he tried, unsuccessfully, to market his double-decker bicycle, will they be interested in his siblings, those who never took part in the hang gliding?

Hour after hour I wrestled with the small decisions, deciding that some moments could be dramatized and made larger while others had to be condensed down to a sentence.

Over the years, readers have asked, "Wasn't that a hard book to write?" and it's always clear what they mean; they are referring to the deaths of our two sons. The truth is, as a writing task, those portions were not difficult at all. I wrote fast and from the heart, and I cried a lot and became choked up and could hardly breathe, and the words poured out and my keyboard became wet with tears, but the text appeared the way it was meant to be and never had to be changed.

The hard decisions concerned the lesser incidents that seemingly didn't "count."


THERE WERE OTHER ISSUES—LIKE what do with my villains. The story contained several, all recognizable in the community. Aware that publishers don't wish to be sued (or me either), I decided that no villain could wear his own body, or claim his own name, or live where he actually lived. Everything was changed except what the evildoer actually *did*. If one of those bad guys wanted to take me to court and tell the jury, "That was me, all right, I did those things she said I did," I'd take my chances.

Nobody ever sued.

Harder to deal with were critical passages about my own family. How honest did I dare be? Students ask me about this all the time. "If I tell the truth, my mother will kill me." Or, "My son will never speak to me again."

Each family is different. I survived by being painfully honest— compassionate but honest. I tried to explain *why* certain people did what they did, like my mother-in-law's incessant interference with our son, Bobby, bordering on sabotage, but all done out of love. Or my husband erupting into an out-and-out fistfight with his oldest son, the product of sheer exasperation. I even described how clumsily they fought, and how the two of them fell against the plate glass window in the family room and how the window exploded and the whole north wall came crashing down—and how disgusted I was with both of them.

Years later I asked my editor, "When did you decide to buy the book?" and she said, "When I got to the fistfight between your husband and son. It was so *honest*."

Some families can survive painful scrutiny and others can't. As a writer you have to decide whether your book will cost you more than you'll gain if it's published. I always wondered how Joan Crawford's daughter fared at home after she wrote, *Mommie Dearest*.

SINCE MY AGENT, PATTY Teal, was no longer interested in trying to market *Downwind,* I had to find a new agent. I never minded that she'd given up. If I'd been my agent, I'd have given up too. Of all the people remotely connected to that book, only I was crazy enough to keep going. The rest—my friends, my critique group, my husband, my agent—had washed their hands of it long since. The project had begun to look like one writer's absurd and endless obsession.

What nobody knew, except me, was that the manuscript had actually become pretty good. How *would* they know? Not one of them wanted to read it again—even one more time.

By the late '80s, now a little desperate, I was sending the book out to anyone who seemed even slightly interested—editors I met at writers' conferences, editors I met at the ABA (American Book Seller's Association, as it was called then), agents whose names I chose from source books. I remember once collaring a prestigious editor at the ABA, a grandmotherly lady who positively sparkled, and how she stood in an aisle and talked to me at length, listening to my story with what I could only describe as rapt attention. She told me to mail the book to her at her office, and of course I did, immediately.

It was shocking to see how fast the manuscript came back, and how brief, cold, and impersonal a "No" could be—which simply could not have represented the mind-set of the gracious lady I'd met in person.

That rejection was a stark, memorable lesson. We all "know" it, but now I **really** knew, that the best editors are so insulated by a layer of first-readers, that no unagented individual has the slightest hope of breaking through, no matter how dazzled the editor may have seemed in person.

Never had the need for an agent seemed clearer.

Eventually *Downwind* was taken on by a top agent, Richard Curtis, whose enthusiasm was so keen he gave me chills. His voice was deep and rich, and when he explained how much he liked the manuscript, I nearly swooned. By then it had been nine years in the making.

But first he wanted the "Chris" portions printed in a different font and type size to assure a clear distinction between the two voices. He also felt it needed a new title because *Downwind* sounded so negative.

The typestyle change was brilliant, so vital to clarity it was a wonder only he had thought of it. Soon he came up with a new name: *Mother of Eagles.*

I still remember where I stood, and how hard I tried not to blurt out my reaction, which was that he'd just suggested the ickiest title I'd ever heard . . . and how words suddenly flew into my head and instead I blurted out, "How about *Higher Than Eagles?*"

Fortunately, that was it for the title. We agreed amicably and Richard Curtis went to work.

WE BOTH THOUGHT HE'D sell the book easily.

Instead, he was never able to sell it at all. When he finally gave up with a sigh, Curtis said, "A few years ago I could have sold this book in a heartbeat. I'd have had no trouble at all. I'm sorry, Maralys. It's a very good book. But this is a terrible market." His discouragement echoed in every word.

I thanked him, and that was the end of our relationship.

Where to turn next? By now I'd moved my rejection slips into a bigger envelope. I'd even re-read the book with an eye to revamping it yet again, but except for a few small changes the story seemed about as good as I could make it.

Rob was still saying, "Why don't you just *finish* the damned thing?"

and I said, "I *have* finished it," and I was thinking how Eric and Bobby had lived with me through all those many re-writes, how each time I began anew they'd appeared in my study once more. I could actually see their faces. But now the book was finished, and they'd died one last time. And I couldn't tell Rob how final it felt to say good-bye to them forever.

But you couldn't keep writing one book all the rest of your life.

Rob said, "Then write something else."

Well, that was obvious.

But about that book I had an attitude. I was **never** going to give up on selling it, not as long as I was still alive . . . as long as I could still buy stamps and drive it to the post office. But, like an orphan left to fend for itself, the most immediate problem was finding someplace new for the poor thing to go.

MEANWHILE, IF I INTENDED to keep writing, and I did, another change of genres was inevitable.

## Chapter Twenty-One

# Re-writing

Years ago an author in Vermont summed up perfectly the issue of re-writing books. I don't recall his name but his words will remain part of what I say to students. He stood at a podium talking to a roomful of authors—though I felt he was speaking directly to me. He waved his hands in a gesture of helplessness. "An author never finishes a book. He just abandons it."

We all laughed, and I thought of the few books I'd written and sold by then, and the book I'd been writing for years and God knows, might still be writing a few years hence; that author's words reverberated throughout my psyche, because I knew the book of my heart would have to be abandoned soon. I'd have to give up on it. Let it go. Send it off once more to the people in power.

Still, you're never sure it's perfect, even after dozens of readings, each accompanied by word changes and tinkering. It's merely the best you could do that day. So you finally, and reluctantly, send it away.

The depressing part is, if the book comes back, and it probably will, you'll see all the changes you should have made in that last go-around. Sentences that stick out and fail to fit the rhythmic flow, others lying lifeless with eyes rolled back, contributing nothing. Ordinary words that scream to be replaced by splashier words. Whole scenes that appear flaccid, creating no visual images. My God, how could you have mailed it off like that, when it still needed so much work? No wonder they didn't buy it.

There are few rules to be offered about re-writing, besides the fact that it's essential, a critical part of the writing process. Besides my husband, I don't know any authors who write such polished script that their first effort gleams with a surgical luster and feels flawless.

Yet even this precept gets broken occasionally. Once in a while you find yourself sliding into a zone, usually after you've been at the computer a long time and written and struggled and sweated for what seems like hours. As you approach this zone, the words suddenly start spewing out, faster and then faster; they arrive by themselves and fit together beautifully, and you're hardly working at all but the page is filling up anyway, as though you're merely a conduit, a spectator. When you're finished you look at the stuff and it's good.

And it still looks good the next day. And tinker as you might, you can't find anything to change. A word or two but that's all. And it still looks wonderful two weeks later.

The zone is a gift from heaven. I call it a reward for endless muscular work. Though I surely deserve to be zoned often, in fact it occurs only rarely, and always on an afternoon when I'm due momentarily at the dentist's. It's like a heavenly dream, the kind where part of you wants to go on sleeping and never wake up.

Unfortunately, the zone is the exception.

Re-writing is the norm. As surely as you're putting down brand-new sentences, you will come back to those same sentences an hour or a day later and find ways to make them better.

If I were a new author, I'd be asking, *How do I make my work better? How do I know what needs fixing? What tells me the work isn't right?*

Time, I think. Time and thousands of hours of writing. And endless reading of other good writers.

There are no shortcuts to the process. Even when you've read good books all your life, you'll be amazed at the difference between your first efforts and the words of polished professionals. You'll see a difference, all right, but you won't know what it is. You'll read what you've written and love it at first, but a day later you won't love it as much, and finally you'll like it only a little. You'll realize these are not lines somebody will keep by his typewriter to inspire him. Soon, even in your own head, the piece won't stand up to repeated scrutiny. Most of it you'll throw away.

The process of re-writing grows as you grow, it progresses through stages.

In the beginning, you re-write to straighten out your grammar, to untangle awkward sentences. You re-write to take the confusion out of a story, so it moves smoothly from one episode to another. You polish to remove unnecessary or duplicated words in one spot and add meaning in another.

In the next stage, with your mind no longer tangled in clumsy verbiage, you're looking for vividness, for immediacy. You're striving to make meaning jump off the page. You're trying to create word pictures. You're expanding scenes to build drama.

At a more advanced stage, when the basics are under control and you can craft a decent sentence nearly every time and your word pictures are good and your drama fairly rich, you polish for flair, for creative ways to "spin" ordinary ideas.

By the end, you're polishing for magic.

Re-writing is like sculpting. I imagine myself working in a fine white clay, as beautiful as marble, able to shape it any way I choose, paring down the places that stick out, adding chunks where it's too lean, trimming delicately as it hardens . . . making a thousand changes, some so small they're hardly noticeable, yet important enough so they'll flag me down when they're wrong.

You cannot reach the eventual shape of the piece even after many re-workings. Oh, no. You trim away a bit and stand back and look it over, and you press in more clay to round out a sunken spot and stand back once more and study the results, and you keep trimming and fleshing out, adding bits here and pulling away other bits there, forming, molding, feathering—assessing the total effect until you finally like it and no more can be done.

Sometimes as you re-write, you'll notice that your first word choices turned out to be right after all. That impulsive blurting you assumed was wrong, really wasn't wrong, it was instinct, the writer's mind choosing the most graceful arrangement of words. Re-writing implies having the courage to trust your first, your most basic instincts.

Re-writing also means defending your work against the pillaging of well-meaning but too-ardent critiquers. It means recognizing that your style is your style and tampering with it even a little can possibly dull it down. It means knowing your words aren't written in cement, but on the other hand, your judgment as a reader is there to be trusted, and trust it you must.

RE-WRITING HAS ITS PECULIAR aspects. I, for one, learned long ago that I cannot tell how my work reads until I see it cleanly written with no changes. All my early attempts at re-writing—interlineations, sentences scribbled down the sides of a page and around the corner— were almost useless and told me nothing. None of it could be accurately assessed—not until I'd typed it in final form.

Which meant that way back before my first computer, all those painstaking, penned-in changes I imagined were brilliant and tangy and worthy of Hemingway, translated into sentences with a funny "feel," to them, as though they'd been glued together with cream-of-wheat. However brilliant I imagined the work had become, when cleanly typed it still stumbled and bumped along dismayingly . . . and I had to change it yet again.

Don't ask me how this could be. I don't know.

Enough to say that in my typewriter days, the larger part of my writing hours went to re-typing sentences and paragraphs so I'd know how they read. And then wasting more time fixing and re-typing once again.

Now that we have computers with screens, **everything** appears cleanly written, even after you've picked away at the piece and changed your mind endlessly. Writing hours now go to creation instead of busy work.

That said, I've learned that some authors can't assess their work on the screen either, but must print out hard copies to grasp fully what they have.

HERE ARE A FEW lines from the movie critique section of *The New Yorker* that struck me as extraordinary. I would love to ask this writer whether the words came to him easily or only as the result of grueling effort—or something in between. In any case, effortless is how they appear.

The piece is called *Bombs Away,* and it's a review of the movie *Pearl Harbor,* written by Anthony Lane. He says in part, "This is one of those long but bitty movies in which actors get their characters handed out like parcels of rations—a nervous tic for you, a knot of frustration for him. Evelyn and the other nurses are delighted with a gang of fliers who are assigned to Pearl Harbor; we get Gooz . . . a fellow of few words and many bruises, Red . . . who has a comedy stammer that you just know will kick in at a vital juncture, and, above all, Rafe's friend Danny. Oh-oh.

*"The moment he appeared, looking shy and sculpted, my radar picked up a large, aggressive plot twist steaming in from the Northwest."*

If I could ever, just once, write something as vivid as those few words about a plot twist, I would feel I'd arrived in writer's heaven. I'd know I was capable of creating magic.

And magic is what it takes to sell a book.

## Chapter Twenty-Two

# HIGHER THAN EAGLES

BY NOW, I HONESTLY believed *Higher Than Eagles* contained elements of magic.

Surely the judgment of a top agent had to count for something, there had to be an editor in some large or small publishing house who would validate Richard Curtis's belief in the project.

My book was like a comely girl looking for a husband. She'd never get a marriage proposal wrapped around a brick flying through her bedroom window. She had to be **out there**, she had to be *seen*.

For a while, every spare minute when I wasn't doing something else, I was sending out *Higher Than Eagles*. In only three years it went to twenty-two editors plus assorted agents.

Just recently, in doing research for this book, I pulled from my file cabinet a big, tattered manila envelope full of rejection letters and glanced at the lists of publishers printed carefully on the outside, with send-off dates and return dates. It was like looking at old x-rays of broken bones or cancerous growths. The evidence of defeat was *so right there*, methodically recorded in a spirit of hope until the last return date was entered. I read a few of the letters, and even then, when it was no longer reasonable to feel defeated or futile, I inexplicably felt bad anyway, wondering how I'd kept going in the face of so many

Nos, with ultimate success never certain . . . and whether I could still persist quite as doggedly today.

I'm not sure I could.

The envelope was not like my shoebox. I realized there was nothing about it of symbolism or triumph, only an aura of sadness, an emanation that was almost spooky in the way it could still conjure up feelings of futility.

I dragged the envelope down to my class and held it open so my students could see those dozens of letters inside (why, I'm not sure, unless it was to share my angst with people I was certain would understand), and I began to realize as the students stared blankly into the gaping interior that they didn't understand after all, because none of them had gone through it.

I was alone in my feelings; only I fully grasped what the worst part of publishing was all about, that it is **so** not-automatic, that it can take hundreds of tries before that one publisher, the single leaf in a forest of leaves, is found, that even if a work is superb, the right leaf might never be located.

My students didn't understand how I could still feel upset and discouraged and queasy about something that *almost didn't happen*, about a book that, except for an unexpected miracle, might never have sold at all.

Here I was, with all this weighty proof of the "almost-wasn't," and they obviously saw only the miracle. One of them said brightly, "Well, you sold it, anyway," as though the final outcome was all that mattered, and that my discouraging journey of fourteen years had been kind of incidental.

I realized it takes walking the route yourself and feeling every sharp and punishing stone before you can appreciate the frail, thin line separating "sold" from "unsold"—the almost accidental crossing of that line that finally makes the journey worthwhile.

AS POINTLESS AS IT seemed to approach editors directly, you had to trust those who appeared at writers' conferences and let you pitch your manuscript, then asked for a direct submission. Which is how I happened to send the book to Jim Wade, Senior Editor of

Crown Books. His rejection letter, when it came, was so astonishing I still remember most of the words. "This is a powerful book about dreams and loss," he wrote, "about the force that drives the human spirit beyond the edges of risk. I know that it is made up of the lives of your family, this extraordinary story."

I read the letter and sat there blinking in surprise. I felt breathless, almost overcome. How could this letter be considered a rejection? Why weren't his words engraved forever on the jacket cover? How had he managed to encapsulate the spirit of the book better, even, than I?

At the end he wrote, "Keep trying. Don't let this discourage you in any way. I don't have to tell you there is a remarkable story here—you know. Make this dream happen too. Don't give up."

At the time I could only think, If you loved it so much, why in this wide world didn't you buy it?

Now, MANY YEARS LATER, I believe James Wade *wanted* to buy it, that left to his own inclinations he *would* have bought it, but that he was constrained by a bottom line committee that allowed him no choice. All he could do was pour out his soul on the typewriter, hoping to give me the strongest possible push.

I've come to believe that this happens often in publishing . . . that individual editors fall in love with certain manuscripts which, before the '80s, they would have had the authority and the backing to buy. But once publishing houses began vanishing into conglomerates that were controlled by non-literary, non-reading bean counters, freedom for editors all but vanished under the weight of the fearsome bottom line. As Michael Korda, long-time senior editor for Simon and Schuster writes in *Another Life,* "It is hardly surprising that most publishing houses are now run by people who would just as soon climb Everest without oxygen as edit a book (or, in some cases, *read* one.)"

THE EDITORS WERE SLOWLY drowning me. Each rejection from an editor was another stone tied to my waist, dragging me under. Sometimes I still had the long view, that one day these letters would seem almost laughable. Other moments it seemed I was going under for the third time.

Though I'd been in sporadic touch with Editor Saul Cohen (who'd left Prentice-Hall and was now an agent), and though, over the years, he'd turned down three different renditions of *Eagles,* each time without encouragement, I asked him to look at this one last version. He said he would.

This time, to my astonishment, the tone of his letter was so different it was almost a pæan and matched the spirit and words of Jim Wade. He ended the letter by saying flatly, "I'm putting a $35,000 floor under your book."

Gripping his letter in awe, I floated across the house to the kitchen, and when Rob was nowhere to be seen I began, from longstanding habit, to clear away the dishes. Then I stopped. *Why am I doing this, I thought, grubbing around in the kitchen . . . when I'm worth $35,000!*

In my mind it was all so clear: the money was in my bank account and the maids would be coming soon. I closed the dishwasher, pushed the plates aside, and walked away.

When Rob finally appeared he said, "How come the kitchen's a mess?" And somehow he never saw the maids as clearly as I did.

THOUGH SAUL COHEN TRIED even longer and harder than Richard Curtis, the end result was the same. Editors made thin excuses, often spewing out the same trite phrases that had come winging back to me when I was the agent, and then to Richard when he was the agent. "This isn't right for our house." Only now, instead of saying "Dear Richard," they said, "Dear Mr. Cohen," which came as a shock. Saul Cohen, operating out of Connecticut, obviously did not have the close personal, "Let's meet for lunch" relationships with editors that might have made the difference.

Then I thought, *Fat lot of good those personal relationships did*, because Richard Curtis couldn't sell the book with **everyone** calling him Richard.

What to do next? For a while I did nothing.

Well, not quite. What I did was forget the memoir and begin writing another, a wholly different, kind of book.

THE IDEA FOR A party game book came about one day when I pulled out the long, very long, drawer that starts in our bedroom hall and slides for miles under the stairs, a drawer big enough to hold a body. The drawer was crammed with party games . . . with instructions for games, with props for games, with sheets all made up for games, with lists of past parties and all the games we'd played. Quite haphazard, not organized at all because the drawer was so big you could just keep throwing things into it forever.

As I stood there pondering, I thought, *Here's a book*. Surely there must be other adults like Rob and me who dislike cocktail parties where everyone stands around drinking and shouting into each others' faces, and where, if you're lucky, you can talk to two or three people in a whole evening (if they can hear you), and where you come home exhausted without having had much fun.

The two of us never gave that kind of party.

On the other hand, Rob and I shared endless memories of hilarious evenings where adults played games—either at our house, or the Presbyterian Church, or the homes of other churchees.

From our earliest party-giving days, we'd discovered that games are nothing if not a magical way to learn more about your friends. They are like profiling, like the couch in a psychologist's office. No one can hide from a game's probing eyes; it reveals personality down through several layers. With clever games you find out in a hurry who is imaginative, who is sneaky, who is brilliant, who is wildly competitive, who has a fund of useless knowledge, and who has the great sense of humor.

For us, the most important, the paramount feature of games was laughter. The games-evenings were the nights when you'd laughed so much your face felt permanently creased and you came home feeling light, as though little strings were floating you above the earth, as though everyone you knew was a pal and nothing would ever really annoy you again.

IT DIDN'T TAKE MUCH staring at the game drawer to give me the idea: why not write a party game book for **adults**?

Before I started, I knew what I'd do. This wouldn't be a mere collection—it would be more. All the rationale behind party games would be included, plus the knowledge we'd accumulated over the years about what "works" and what doesn't. Among these would be the observation that the hostess who suddenly springs on her unsuspecting guests the bright suggestion, "Let's play charades!" is usually doomed.

Guests who come unprepared for games seldom respond well if a Sudden Inspiration, especially **that game**, is dropped on their heads at 11:00 p.m., when they're already yawning. The very word "Charades" has acquired a taint. It implies coercion, an energetic young hostess bulldozing her tired guests into brightening up and trying to appear smart.

No. No. No. This would not be a book about pushing guests around, especially into charades. In fact Rob was pressing to call it, *The No-Charades Party Game Book.*

KNOWING A NON-FICTION BOOK could be sold on a couple of good chapters plus a detailed outline, I wrote a proposal (I finally knew what one was), and asked Patty Teal if she'd like to sell it, and she said she would.

Patty worked hard on that sale, and after a while she brought me an offer from an important publishing house, with terms you'd call skimpy. I'd get $5,000 up front and no royalties.

No royalties? What if the book took off and people everywhere wanted to buy it? No royalties?

At first it seemed like such a meager offer neither of us had much enthusiasm, but by the time I said, "Okay, Patty, let's go for it," my proposal had been rejected enough times so the offer's bad odor was wearing off.

Not long after I signed the contract and before the editors had begun to work with me, the publisher reneged. It wasn't *the book* they ran out on, it was the *idea,* because no book had yet reached them.

"Since you've already got the money," Patty said, "they can't take it back," and she explained that the advance was mine—at least until the book sold somewhere else.

"So let's sell it somewhere else," I said, and she said she'd try, and I said,

"Why don't I help you?" because it seemed the fair thing to do.

THE TWO OF US came up with a plan that could only represent the collaboration of a couple of nuts who were best friends. We agreed that I'd send out query letters to editors, and she'd send out the proposal to any who responded positively.

She never dreamed I would send out 137 letters.

Actually, in the beginning, neither did I. It just happened, a response to defeat that by then was so much a part of my character, such an immutable mix of German stubbornness and the *Reader's Digest*, that it was taking on the aspects of an inherited disease.

I still remember how I felt. *By damn it's a good book and I won't give up.*

A few editors wanted to see more, and among those few, at least half turned us down with high praise; but the final word was still No.

Patty and I wouldn't give up.

The world by then was full of desperate authors coming up with crazy ideas for selling books, some even more bizarre than ours. The two of us decided to go to New York City, rent a hotel room, and invite all the important editors to come for a night of party games, thus proving how "right," how very entertaining, adult games could be.

It never occurred to me until later that we might have proved something altogether different. Had we served liquor, and we might have, it was possible that we'd have found ourselves with a whole roomful of *drunk editors.*

What a deadly scenario *that* would have been.

It wouldn't have taken many boozy brains to dampen our games until our brilliant idea blurred right before everyone's eyes.

PATTY AND I ACTUALLY made New York plans. But before we did anything concrete, Rob suggested I approach Price-Stern-Sloan in Los Angeles, because they were the publishers of merry little books called *Mad Libs.*

"I wish I could," I said. "But they've already turned me down."

"Why?"

"Who knows? Editors never give you reasons." Still, with nothing to lose, I called them anyway, and got through to Vice-President Nick Clemente, who agreed to meet me in person.

Mr. Clemente and I hit it off. He asked if I'd brought the manuscript, which I had, and he suggested I leave it with him for a second look.

Eight months later, with Patty valiantly negotiating the best possible terms, a *royalty sale,* Price-Stern-Sloan bought the book.

IT WAS ONLY AFTER the book went into production that I gathered the nerve to ask Mr. Clemente, "How did you happen to buy a book you'd already turned down?"

"Pretty simple," he said. "The first time we asked the older editors if they played party games, and they all said no. The second time we asked the younger editors, and most of them said yes."

Another odd thing about that project. When I was midway into it, working hard over final drafts with an editor, she said to me one day in a tone of genuine surprise, "You can really *write*!"

NONE OF MY BOOK sales worked out any better than *Fun Games for Great Parties.* Price-Stern-Sloan produced a beautiful book, so colorful on the outside and so bold and blue on the inside, that it went through several reprints, remained on the shelves for eight years, and ultimately sold more than 23,000 copies.

All those years Patty and I had the fun of crowing to each other about the royalty statements.

No author would have minded genre-hopping into a book like that.

WHEN I BEGAN MY next project, I shifted directions once more. Once again I was feeling my way in strange territory, where research was the foundation and character counted for everything.

Creating believable characters loomed large, of course, in the romances. But great characters mattered even more to the plot of a techno-thriller.

And so the next chapter is devoted to **Characterization**, an author's tricks for creating real people on the printed page.

## Chapter Twenty-Three

# Characters That "Live"

Nothing is more vital to a novel, or trickier to create from scratch, than a living character—the kind with a face you can picture and little quirks you can describe . . . someone you swear you've known. More than twists of plot, more than realistic setting, readers remember the strong individuals in a story. They come away feeling they know personally the gritty Scarlett O'Hara, the sweetly-patient Meggie Cleary, the complex and unpredictable Rhett Butler, the wise and gentlemanly Atticus Finch.

The same can be said for characters in memoirs—the cruel step-mother, for instance, in *Fallen Leaves*. But memoir authors have a distinct advantage. It's not terribly difficult to portray people you already know. Your brain keeps them on tap for instant recall. It's easy to depict on paper your elderly grandfather's sad, patient face, his arthritic walk, the hands that wobble on a cane, his stout assurances, "You needn't worry about me. I'm doing okay."

For my own memoir, I didn't have to work at re-creating Ruth, my mother-in-law. I could hear her saying, "Oh, my stars!" as she clapped a dismayed hand over her mouth. I could picture her wriggling out of her old Cadillac . . . then, when one of our children so much as frowned, I could see her anguished face as she cried out, "Chris! Bobby!

Are you hungry? My lands, they must be hungry, poor dears, here, let me get them something, they've got to eat, oh, those poor, dear children, they're hungry!" And then she'd be tearing open a brown paper bag and pulling out jars of carrot juice and little health-food candy bars.

I can still picture her hobbling to the front door, and hear my four-year-old grandson, Dane, watching her walk and chirping brightly, "I can do the old thing," and how, on his four-year-old legs, he hobbled along behind her.

The same went for our son, Bobby, whom I could picture whenever I tried, sitting on the cold cement of our garage, hair in his eyes, greasy hands busy with odd bicycle parts, and a freaky, double-decker bicycle propped nearby. I could hear his voice crying out to his father, "This isn't playing, Dad, just because I like what I do. It's not playing! It isn't! What I do is important! You'll see! Someday this will amount to something. Just wait!"

For a memoir, all an author need do is write down what her inner eye sees. So yes, it's almost unfair, because producing characters for a memoir isn't so much creation as transcription.

NOVELS ARE WHERE THE work starts. Fashioning living, breathing characters for novels is more than a challenge, it's one of those sticky, puzzling, sometimes off-putting jobs, because with fiction you're forced to make it all up, you're basically starting with nothing.

Well . . . maybe you are and maybe you're not.

Many an author has "borrowed" the personality of someone he knows . . . or maybe the combined personalities of several someones.

Which is one way to start. Let's say you've got the germ of a plot, about a tough cop who can handle all kinds of felons on the street but has no idea how to cope with his own wayward son. Let's say his instincts as a policeman collide with his instincts as a father.

This is a man the author must quickly get to know.

The author might draw on characteristics of his own father, as Pat Conroy did for *The Great Santini,* (A novel which rang exceedingly true, because the author had such keen insights into the hero, who of course was patterned after the man who'd raised him.)

The writer might use a few of his dad's small, personal habits in sketching the policeman character: the cop drinking his coffee in great gulps, nervously fingering his belt—or gun—combing his hair straight back from a deep widow's peak, talking right through others on the telephone.

These are just ideas that pop up as I try to create a man I haven't really known. But his qualities, as invented, will certainly affect the plot. As the character and the plot intersect, some of these qualities may need modification . . . or more likely, the plot will be changed to fit the author's view of this very strong character.

Except in romance novels, few authors lean heavily on physical description as an integral part of character. Unless blonde jokes affect the heroine's life, it doesn't matter whether she's blonde or brunette, short or tall.

For most books, physical characteristics are important only when they matter a great deal to the character himself: a plump heroine who suffers inwardly, a too-short man who feels a need to prove himself, a grossly overweight entertainer who tries to make light of embarrassing efforts to pull himself off a couch.

Still, extremes in bodily proportions might be employed as one defining element of character. If an author were trying to design a clichéd "bad guy" she might have noticed how many street criminals are described on news reports as five-seven to five-ten. And how few (I can't remember any) as six-four or above.

The stereotypical criminal, then, would be short, slight, and pugnacious. But a novelist's twist on the cliché might be a criminal who is six-feet-six. Think of the plot possibilities . . . the measures that a near-giant would have to take to conceal his identity. A ski mask wouldn't do it. In fact, nothing would adequately hide a man who towers over most other humans. As of this writing, some wonder how a giant like Osama bin Laden has so far managed to escape detection.

In designing unique character, we look for life's formative experiences. As obvious as it is that a Harvard law school graduate wouldn't see life the same as an immigrant laborer picking strawberries, between these extremes are a range of subtleties so vast that an author's choices are endless.

When you're creating a character, you get to play God. You pick the protagonist's school, his parents, his neighborhood, his siblings, his position in the family, his hobbies, his educational level, his friends, his life's experiences. And then you decide which to twist and which to make clichéd.

Even as you craft this character, say, a scientist gone bad, you choose the school that educated him, but you also select the factors that soured him. Why would a man devoted to pure science and all that implies—honesty, respect for principle, devotion to proof, love of facts—choose to cast aside all the accepted mores in his profession and become dishonest?

Would this be a gradual process, or would it happen all at once? Would you see the character slowly eroding, one gray choice at a time, or would he suddenly turn black?

As his creator, you would look for schisms in his background . . . a science-teacher father who purports to live ethically, but issues secret, defamatory reports on his fellow teachers. A mother who pretends to love an offspring she secretly despises.

You might even design for this unhappy man some kind of grim life experience: a dying daughter who needs an unaffordable operation (a new liver), and a drug company who approaches him on the side, willing to pay handsomely for "skewed" laboratory test results on rats. Maybe the man wouldn't have to fudge much—just a little. Maybe he had a sister who died years earlier from the same disease that is now wracking his daughter.

The more you write about this character, the more will come to you and the better you'll understand him. While you may not grasp the whole man at the beginning of the novel, by the end you'll know him intimately.

Often, visualizing a character you've never met is close to impossible. I decided long ago I couldn't create believable characters unless I could see them on my mental screen. Sometimes the best way to accomplish that was to visualize the likeliest movie star. In my mind's eye, the cop could resemble Tommy Lee Jones.

For one of my romances I wanted a strong, unyielding, earth-solid person like Gary Cooper, the hero in *High Noon*. I pictured Cooper standing alone in the street facing down his enemies, an impervious man who wouldn't blink in the face of disaster.

Using Gary Cooper as my mental image, I created a hero who felt so real to me that I always knew how he'd react in any situation. Every time a plot question arose, I pictured my protagonist standing bravely in the street, and I knew how he'd behave. The image was so strong it carried me through the novel, translating repeatedly into consistent behavior.

I knew I'd succeeded when a friend read the romance and said, "Your hero reminds me of Gary Cooper."

Some authors cut pictures out of magazines and paste them near their computers, hoping to assure a strong mental image.

If picturing a face seems a superficial approach to defining character, think of the qualities that leap out at us when we look at the face of Abraham Lincoln: integrity; grit; abiding sadness; a grinding sense of duty; deep compassion. When I see Lincoln's face, I think of the cabinet member who, early in his presidency, scorned him for his country-boy background, but said after his death, "Now he belongs to the ages."

BECAUSE IT'S SO VITAL to get inside the head of a character, to "feel" her from the inside, it helps to write her autobiography. I've done this many times as I tried to create characters I'd never known.

The following might be the first person account of a driven tennis champ: "I am Kelly Smith, and I grew up hating my father. Dad was a failed athlete, kicked out of college for cheating. He thought he could relive his glory days through me. On my sixth birthday, he forced me to start playing tennis. At first I liked the attention. Dad took me to the courts, drilled me endlessly, and drove me to tournaments. But then he started yelling when I called good balls in. He became a maniac. He found ways to hate my opponents and taught me to hate them too. He raised me on anger, getting red in the face when I blew a point, calling me "Wuss" when I lost a match. All my teenage years Dad punished me for failure. And now his anger boils inside me. It's *his* competitive spirit I can't shake, *his* drive to win at all costs that has altered my psyche. The gentle part of me was smothered years ago; it died when I ran away from home and he hauled me back. When I smash balls at an opponent, I am really smashing them at my father."

The mere act of dreaming up Kelly's story and letting her tell it in her own words gives an author the sense that she IS Kelly. Which is key to understanding why Kelly turned out the way she did.

As you're designing a protagonist, you'll be looking for at least one key trait: seriousness; integrity; energy; light-heartedness; competitiveness; zaniness; moodiness; fairness; belligerence; steadfastness. The list is endless.

But keep in mind that key traits are a character's best **and worst** traits. Which holds true for real life. The woman who's so ambitious she overcomes all obstacles to become CEO of Gateway is also the woman whose drive for success can be infuriating to those who know her best. The light-hearted character with a gift for amusing his friends may also be so laid back he forgets to pay the bills. The sympathetic woman who shows compassion for the lowliest worker in a car wash (as did my mother-in-law), also gushed and emoted over everyone in the family and drove us all nuts. The brilliant lawyer admired for his insights can also be the arrogant character who always knows too much.

Strangely, a character can even have too much integrity. I know such a man and at times I want to yell at him to loosen up.

Each of these traits has its positive and negative connotations, depending on which descriptive word you choose. The dark side of my own key trait, persistence, is sometimes called obsession.

The author's challenge is to explore key traits in both their best and worst connotations, and to make the character appear rounded by recognizing that his most admirable characteristics are those which also do him in.

During the course of most novels, important characters change. They modify their key traits, they gain insight into themselves and others, they make decisions they wouldn't have made at the story's start. Without character change, a novel spins in one place.

In my memoir, *Eagles*, our son, Bobby, changed markedly, from a stubborn young man without purpose, to an innovator and champion in the field of hang gliding, where stubbornness was useful and became grit. Though his key trait never entirely changed, by the end of his life, it had softened and become reasonable—even as his sense of purpose grew. He was easier to live with, had greater understanding of those around him. Change marked other important characters. By the end of the book, Bobby's impatient father had developed insight, empathy . . . and yes, a modicum of patience.

During the course of my techno-thriller, *Scatterpath*, desperate circumstances force my hero to change from a by-the-books NTSB investigator into an obsessed man who was willing to circumvent Safety Board rules to catch a murderer that only he believed existed.

IN CHAPTER NINE, I mentioned briefly how character is revealed in a book: by what the character says, does, and thinks. And by a fourth method—what others in the novel say or think about him.

Of the four techniques, the last is the easiest; it's amazingly simple to have one character define another for the benefit of the reader.

More difficult is crafting the dialogue that sets a character apart and makes him distinct from other same-sex characters. While regional accents, like a Southern accent or Western drawl, are only minimally useful in a novel (if used too much they become tedious), other, subtler, speech patterns distinguish one man or woman from another: the clipped speech versus the leisurely syntax; the use of direct, hard-hitting, versus indirect language. And such attitude differences as impatience versus acceptance . . . enthusiasm versus fault-finding . . . reasoned versus hasty opinions.

Colorful expletives set characters apart—though to many of us, falling back on the "F" word as the all-purpose expletive is the copout of the lazy and unimaginative writer.

IT'S EASIER TO PORTRAY a protagonist by what he does, because here the reader can't be fooled. The character either does or doesn't do things that are kind, selfish, cruel, thoughtful, generous, stupid.

And the contrast between what a character is doing or saying and what he's thinking provides the final, incisive clue to his personality. A man might be saying, "You look lovely in that dress, Charmaine," but thinking, *Where did you get it—the Salvation Army?*

Sidney Sheldon was the master of sketching character by offering inner thoughts that contrasted wildly with what the person was saying. In *Windmills of the Gods*, he lets us into the head of the heroine, Mary, who has just become Ambassador to Romania. The Romanian president takes Mary's hand and says, "'I hope you will grow to love our country, Madam Ambassador.' He massaged her hand.

"'I'm sure I will.' *He thinks I'm just another pretty face*, Mary thought grimly. *I'll have to do something about that.*"

Having arrived at novel-writing through screen-writing, Sheldon also crafted brilliant dialogue.

By THE END OF a story, the reader wants to know **why** the protagonist did whatever he did. Which means that throughout the book the author must be aware of motivation. Nobody does anything with zero motivation. We all have reasons for our weird or wonderful or destructive behavior.

In fact, we might even have spiteful reasons for being kind to others and, by contrast, altruistic motives for what appears to be cruelty . . . as for instance, the mother who made headlines by shooting her two dying sons. It's up to the author to find these reasons and make the protagonist believable.

ON THAT NOTE I'D like to end with a real-life character I've thought about often but never understood—a man who'd make a fascinating subject for a novel.

Let's call him David Martin. Martin was in my husband's law school class, a brilliant man who ranked third among that year's graduates. He was on the Law Review staff, respected by everyone. He was also married, with two sons he adored. A devoted family man, he made his own furniture, seemed ready to protect his sons with his life, and on graduation, was offered a job in the area's most prestigious law firm. Martin's parents were decent, solid people, his father a respected doctor.

But suddenly his life flew to pieces. He bought a yacht and an airplane, left his wife for a secretary, quit his law practice, abandoned his children, and eventually lived on the street. The last my husband saw of him, Martin was at my husband's law offices begging for a loan.

Martin died young. None of us could figure out the motivation for his changed life, for why such a gifted man disintegrated until he became, literally, a bum. To an outsider, "drugs" were the obvious reason, but as far as I know, addiction was not part of the scenario.

If I needed such a man, I'd steal aspects of Martin's strange implosion. But as an author, I'd have to invent reasons for his self-destruction, explanations that would make sense to a reader. Martin couldn't sink to the bottom of the pond without strong, logical reasons.

TO THE EXTENT THAT the author knows his characters' key traits, his motivations, and his speech patterns—that he *feels* his characters from the inside and *visualizes* them from the outside—the novel will seem compelling and believable.

## Chapter Twenty-Four

# Finding Ideas—*Scatterpath*

Non-writers, usually the readers in my audiences, sometimes ask, "Where do you get your ideas?" Strangely, my students seldom feel the need for such a question: most of them come to me with ideas pouring out faster than they can type. Ideas are what drove them to writing in the first place.

But to the others I say, "Ideas are everywhere. In the newspapers, in real life situations, everywhere you go. Remembering to jot them down is the problem."

The most graphic example of a book plot springing from a newspaper article is illustrated by my techno-thriller, *Scatterpath*.

With *Higher Than Eagles* pushed to a back burner, and *Fun Games for Great Parties* out in book stores selling better than expected, I was momentarily without a project, though not really looking. And then I happened to see a newspaper headline that inspired a writer's question. The story was about a mysterious blaze in a downtown Los Angeles high-rise, and the banner read: **Arson Investigators to Determine Cause of Fire**.

My immediate writer's question was, How?

I pictured a few hard-hatted men with gloves, boots, and masks, trudging through ankle deep debris picking up charred bits of this and twisted pieces of that and one of them stumbling upon something ordinary, like a melted wastebasket, and saying, "Aha!" . . . as though the answer was clear. As though the guilty wastebasket was stamped with a fireproof confession.

Really.

Where's the logic, I thought, how is it possible to look at something and know when it burned? Blackened objects don't come with numbers, there's nothing that says, The wastebasket burned first, the drapes burned second. It's **all** charred—who's to say where the process began?

THE ARSON HEADLINE CAPTURED my attention, as headlines often do for other writers, What if arson investigators *couldn't* determine the cause of the blaze? What if the fire had been so cleverly set, so well-crafted by a brilliant sociopath, that it left no clues? Wouldn't *that* be a story?

Then it occurred to me that fires weren't terribly exciting, but what I did care about was airplanes and airplane crashes, which provoke similar story questions. How does an investigator determine the cause of a plane crash when the plane's parts litter the ground and every piece is shattered? How does he know whether a crucial component broke in the air or during impact? And what if someone—a mad aeronautical genius—sabotaged a line of aircraft so *nobody* could figure it out?

Was this even possible?

I began making calls. And suddenly I'd started down a new road, ready to write a book of a whole different kind.

THE LADY AT THE FAA switchboard was patient and pleasant. "You don't want us," she said as I explained my mission, "you need to talk to someone at the National Transportation Safety Board. They're the ones who investigate airplane accidents," and she gave me the NTSB's Washington number.

The man at Washington headquarters was similarly cordial. "Since you're from California, why not save yourself long-distance costs and contact the NTSB office in Hawthorne? Somebody there can answer your questions."

Happy Discovery Number One on doing research was just becoming apparent: everyone is eager to help authors write books. Later I would learn that the word "author" was an Aladdin's lamp you could rub and use anywhere. Just utter the word and people drop what they're doing to answer all your questions. I never got used to wielding so much wizardly power.

In Hawthorne the man I asked for wasn't in, but a thoughtful woman said, "I'll let you speak to Jeff Rich. Maybe he can help."

Her suggestion was a turning point, the single best thing that happened during the creation of that book. I just didn't know it yet.

Jeff Rich and I spoke briefly, and he agreed to see me in his office. A few days later I drove to Hawthorne wondering if I was on a harebrained, fruitless mission, and whether there really was a novel to be written about accident investigation and, if there was, could I gather enough expertise to do it?

Jeff Rich met me in the NTSB's small, under-furnished, very plain reception area. He was moderately tall, about my height (5'10"), trim, with dark hair and extremely bright blue eyes. I got the feeling his eyes saw more than mine.

Which, given his job, was probably true.

He led me back to his tiny office, so small that it held only two chairs, though mine was now occupied by a cardboard box full of metal plane parts. There was no place to put the box, so he carefully balanced it on top of another. It was hard to imagine anyone investigating a major trauma in so little space. The room was crammed to the windowsills (if there'd been any windows), with a desk, two file cabinets, a table covered with boxes, and a floor carpeted in stacks of paperwork. Once in, you'd have to leave by backing out.

He smiled apologetically. "Not much room in here," and he seated himself in what was virtually a nest. No bird could have been buried any deeper in the trappings of his life. "Well, how can I help you?" Those bright eyes regarded me quizzically.

"I'm thinking about writing a novel on airplane accidents," I began. "About some maniac bringing down a bunch of planes, which he's able to do because nobody can figure out who he is or why the planes are failing. Is this possible?"

"You mean that we couldn't figure out what was going wrong?" He looked at me thoughtfully for mere seconds, then smiled in polite dismissal. "We could always figure out what was going wrong."

"Oh. Then nobody could sabotage a plane so the sabotage couldn't be detected?"

"That's right."

"So if a plane part broke in the air, you'd always know it happened there and not when the plane hit the ground?"

"Always." Then seeing my look of disappointment, "I'm sorry. But we can tell quite easily whether something broke while the plane was still airborne or later during impact."

I waited to see if he'd continue.

"We look for what we call fracture lines," he said, in the calm tones of a natural-born teacher. "A part that breaks on impact leaves a fracture line. When we put the two halves next to each other, the fracture line goes right across the reconstructed part, so we know it was intact before it hit. If the fracture line doesn't line up when the part is reconstructed, we're sure it broke at some earlier point. It's pretty easy."

"Oh." This wasn't looking good. "Then there's no way a sociopath could sabotage a plane so nobody could figure it out . . . that is, a person like you."

When he shook his head again with that rueful smile, I thought, Well . . . there goes the old book. Nice try, Maralys. Better go home and think of something else.

We both just sat there. I was preparing to leave, to thank him and pick up my purse. If this man, the expert, said planes couldn't be sabotaged, I guessed they couldn't.

But he was still thinking, and since I'd come quite a distance and wasn't especially eager to rush off, I sat and watched him think.

Finally he said, "There might be a way."

I waited silently.

"Yeah, maybe there would be a possibility . . . in the fully automated planes, the computerized aircraft. We call them fly-by-wires. I think those could be sabotaged." He frowned, a million miles away. "If some zealot, some sociopath who was also a computer whiz, got into the computers and created a virus. . . ."

His frown deepened. "But he'd have to make it an erasable virus. Our sociopath would have to program the on-board computers to fail in some way, but only for a brief period, long enough to do damage, but not long enough to be there when investigators started looking. The faulty settings would have to be set in advance, pre-programmed to disappear almost instantly. That way they'd leave no trace."

He stopped talking as additional ideas came to him. "Someone like me would see that the plane had done something bizarre, but with no clues left in the computer, I wouldn't be sure why." He rubbed his chin. "Yeah, I think your maniac could do quite a lot of damage in a fly-by-wire before we'd know what had happened."

He looked up, smiling. He was obviously now caught up in the project. "He might get away with his evil deeds for quite a while."

I smiled back, hoping I didn't appear as greedy as I felt. This was sounding better by the minute. "That's how I'll write it, then. Sabotage by computer. And while I'm at it, would you, by chance . . . I mean, do you have time to help me?"

A brief hesitation. "Not really. But I'll make time." He threw me another rueful smile. "We're all overworked, it comes with this glory job. A little more overworking won't make that much difference."

I felt like jumping up and waltzing him into a dance, but then I'd probably lose him . . . and besides you can't dance in a room where there's no space to turn around, so I stayed cool and merely gave him a warm thanks.

Before I left, I asked where he'd gone to school, and he said UCLA, and when I asked his major, he said English.

Oh perfect, I thought. Perfect.

WE HAD A FEW more meetings in Jeff Rich's Lilliputian cubicle, and I learned more about him and more still about his job. Though he never used the word, the air vibrated with undertones of passion— Jeff's softly stated enthusiasm for his work and all it entailed.

"I take it you like this job," I said, and he said, "I wouldn't do anything else."

"Why? What makes it so great?"

"Importance, I guess. Knowing only you can do it. The undeniable fact that we're saving lives. But it's got variety, too. Each case is different; you never encounter the same scenario twice. You're always learning—you have to. It's a job that requires knowledge in a dozen different areas, so you have no choice but to stay current."

His expression changed subtly. "There are drawbacks, of course. It's hell on relationships. When we get the call, we have to go. Immediately. Middle of the night. During dinner. At the theater. Wherever we are. When you're summoned, you leave, no matter what you're doing. Wives and girlfriends aren't too crazy about that."

"Are you married?"

"No." He smiled. "Never found time. I don't know many guys who've stayed married. In fact I can think of only one. Divorce is pretty much the rule."

"Which means you're married to the job,"

"For now." He didn't seem regretful.

We talked about where I might start the story, with a small, private-plane crash in Tahoe, and he gave me a few ideas: the kind of plane it might be (a Cessna), the sudden storm front that could have obscured the plane's route, the nearby weather stations that might have been contacted.

We parted, agreeing to meet again when I came up with something resembling a plot. At the moment all I had was a tiny, core idea—a seed—and the assurance that the seed was viable and if watered and tended might grow into a story.

I THOUGHT ABOUT JEFF Rich a lot. In my mind, my hero began to live, a man like Rich whose passion for work would eventually destroy everything else in his life. The conflict was already obvious, for what could be more compelling than a man hell-bent on finding a murderous maniac (an important mission? Oh, yes), while at the same time unwittingly bringing down his marriage . . . and eventually destroying even his relationship with a good but skeptical boss.

I began to love the story, for I could *feel* it, even as I felt the drive embodied in Jeff Rich himself. Without knowing it, he'd handed me a real person with real problems that wouldn't easily go away. The conflicts, in fact, would be three-way: my hero pitted against an unknown sociopath, the hero against his wife, the hero against a disbelieving boss—no, more, against a whole hierarchy of colleagues in the NTSB . . . all in the field of aviation, about which I was totally ignorant.

Well, there had to be a fly in there someplace.

A dreaded bugaboo had just come marching onto the scene, the one aspect of writing I'd so far managed to avoid. **Research**.

The idea had always seemed repugnant, suggesting a multitude of boring and unnecessary chores, most to be avoided on grounds that they weren't actually writing but busywork, about as much fun as say, looking up hundreds of obscure annotations in the library.

Okay, I'd heard writers talking, and some had described research as a second love, claiming they found it exciting, at times more engaging than writing.

I never believed them. Instead, I concealed a pitying attitude and a conviction that they weren't at heart writers, they couldn't be, they were well . . . researchers.

If you loved writing, you loved the process. Anything else was just sucking up valuable time.

BUT THAT WAS BEFORE I did any.

That was before I turned into a nut with a notepad and a tape recorder and a phone card and a brand new attitude.

I began to feel like Harriet the Spy. This was getting into places where no ordinary housewife had ever gone, this was learning tidbits that only professional pilots knew, this was earning a pass that makes you a member of a secret society . . . this was, in fact, playing super spy and being first in line to get all the latest, the juiciest, the most titillating information.

LOGICALLY, THE EXPERIENCE LEADS to a chapter devoted entirely to research. The process of creating a book centered on aviation sabotage was so inextricably tied to research that the subject

winds in and out of the next chapter.
Let's consider the next segment an object lesson in research.

## Chapter Twenty-Five

# RESEARCH IN ACTION

JEFF RICH LIKED MY rough plot. At least he liked it well enough so he thought I could start writing. Early in the project as we faced each other uncertainly across his desk, he gave me one of his intense, quizzical looks. "I assume you want this to be real world, right? Something that could actually happen?"

"Of course. It has to be believable."

"If any part is false, you realize, you'll lose the aviation readers."

"I know. I've read a few dumb stories where plates and silverware suddenly flew around the room, and they lost me. So let's agree, Jeff, if anything you read on my pages is not real world, you tell me and I'll fix it or take it out."

"Real world" became our mantra. Our guide. The soul of what we were doing. Ours was not a false aviation setting, but a real one, a journey into the land of What-if, but a journey that even the most critical reader could find possible. Only then would our readers take the ride with genuine interest, with breathless fear, and a sense that, There but for the grace of God goes my plane. . . .

THE WRITING STARTED IN earnest.
And so did the research. What I'd never quite grasped about

research was that, far from being busywork, it adds layers to what you're writing about. How can anyone create a scene about two pilots conversing in a cockpit, for instance, with no idea what's *in* a cockpit, or what the two might physically be doing?

How could I understand the periodic mechanical reviews (they're called "C-checks"), that all airplanes undergo if I'd never personally seen an inspection bay, never saw the airplane hoisted on high, like a whale in a sling, while men with flashlights and tools scramble all over it, peering and probing. How could I discuss airframe manufacturing when I'd never seen an assembly line?

I couldn't.

It was time to visit our local plant. But a friend who worked at what was then McDonnell Douglas warned, "You'll never get in. I've seen a few civic groups come through, but always in bunches, never as individuals. Maybe you could find some kind of group. . . ."

I believed him. Sort of.

At other times I've also believed statements like, *The event is sold out . . . Hospitals don't let writers into operating rooms . . . All the best seats are taken . . . Civilians aren't allowed in the Senate dining room.*

Over the years, I've believed them all. For a while.

But then I've usually asked someone else—which in this case meant calling the Public Relations department of Douglas, expecting nothing, and finding to my surprise that the word "author" cast a spell even in this unlikely, high-powered place. The PR man asked, "What day would you like to come?"

A week later, Mr. Ken Yokimoto met me at one end of the McDonnell Douglas plant and led off on a private tour of the facility, answering questions and letting me stop to examine closer whatever I wanted to see, which included the two of us climbing up into the bloated belly of a giant MD-ll, the first of its kind coming off the production line and destined for Fedex. I looked around that cavernous interior, awestruck by its sheer immensity—*someday this thing will fly*—feeling rather like the first woman on Mars. Nothing offers quite the tingle as invading forbidden territory, or being privy to arcane secrets. Haven't we all wished at times to be the secret observer, the spider under the chair?

An earnest and serious-minded man, Yokimoto seemed in no particular hurry, and in fact, gave the impression that he was mine for the day, while I, in turn, played the cool professional, complete with notepad and questions. I hoped no one would discover I was just a dazzled housewife.

My doubting friend happened to spot us as we strolled along (a great coincidence, since the plant consumed many acres), and he came down from one of those behemoths that filled the room like so many fat-bellied sharks, and stared at me momentarily before he laughed and said, "Well, I see you're here," and he managed not to grill me on how I pulled it off.

I never told him that (in those days), anyone else using the word "author" would have done just as well.

AS VALUABLE AS THE research at McDonnell Douglas proved to be, filling my subconscious with images that could be called up when I needed a climactic chase scene late in the book, a knowledge of physical layouts wasn't enough. I also needed to get inside the head of my villain. How did he ever become so crazy?

None of the research yielded more fascinating insights than the library book I managed to find on sociopaths, and none remained with me more vividly afterwards. The author was clearly shocked by recent trends in our society, in which anchorless and conscienceless children, mostly youngsters who've never bonded with adults, are now killing other children, often as a cold-blooded experiment to "see what happens." A few tiny sociopaths begin murdering as young as ages three or four; almost all are the products of cold, distant, or unbelievably cruel parents.

The childhood years of the most notorious serial killers, men like Charles Manson, the Hillside Strangler, Jeffrey Dahmer, and Ted Bundy, were explored in detail, revealing such monstrous parenting from unfeeling grown-ups it could make you weep. Those who weren't raised by vicious relatives were handed off like batons to a succession of foster homes that contained not a single loving adult.

It was easy to borrow heart-rending incidents from that text and apply them to my airplane saboteur, Rudy Malec, to foist on him childhood events so crushing to his ego (left alone for hours, cold and wet, in his mother's closet), that his twisted mind would eventually seek validation by pitting itself against the best in the NTSB. A friendless soul, as psychopaths usually are, Malec needed something to care about, an animal to lend him a touch of humanity, so I gave him (to my later chagrin), a pet goat.

MY FINAL DISCOVERY ABOUT research, in the highly technical world of aviation, was that you don't have to know **everything** to write a decent scene—only enough to make it believable. A thousand details can be omitted but those that are included must be accurate.

PLOTTING WITHOUT BETTY-JO WAS a new experience, but less daunting when I began to understand, deep down, that good plot flows from strong character. After awhile the story questions arose so logically that the plot more or less tended to itself. Is it possible, I asked, for my NTSB hero to make the wrong decision when he has to choose between his daughter's wedding and a chance to grab the saboteur? (How much agony will he suffer either way?) How much faith should a decent boss put in his best investigator when the man breaks NTSB rules and offers bizarre theories that seem to lack proof? Is a wife justified in leaving a man who is so obsessed he's apparently forgotten he has a family?

As the author, one sees that even good choices can have bad consequences, and we cannot let our hero off too easily.

ALL ALONG I HAD to remember that authors are not allowed to let luck or coincidence dictate the plot. If the boss's niece turns out to be the unexpected pilot of a downed plane, there has to be a *reason*. A very good reason. If our honest hero is unwilling to tell his boss the truth, his thinking must be logical; we can't have readers saying, "Oh, come on, now. Give me a break."

To sum up: No hero can ever be saved because a coconut conveniently drops on his enemy's head.

THROUGHOUT THE YEAR OF writing, Jeff Rich looked over every

page with a critical eye, and kept me supplied with a steady stream of technical and logical information. I was always asking for different scenarios: "Jeff, can you help me design an accident in Las Vegas that's bad but doesn't kill anybody?" "What bizarre thing can happen in the air that scares a seasoned pilot so much he wants to quit?"

As we worked together, I listened for expressions or word combinations that might serve as a title.

One day he happened to mention an NTSB term I'd never heard before. "The lay of the plane after a crash has a name," he said. "It's called the scatterpath."

"Scatterpath!" I cried. "That's it! That's what I'll call the book. I can't think of a better title, can you?"

"Sounds good to me."

BECAUSE OF JEFF I became fascinated with cockpit psychology— with pilots, for instance, who bully and intimidate copilots, making them afraid to speak up (even in dangerous situations, when they need to), which ultimately makes the cockpit unsafe. Knowing the dangers inherent in a one-man cockpit, airlines provide classes in assertiveness training.

It soon became clear that attitude is vital to safety even when the pilot is alone—proved, sadly, by the family of four who died during our project. The pilot/father had already provoked sharp comments from colleagues: "He always pushes to the head of the line. He wants everything now, his way, and fast." Another said, "I watched him in a crisis and decided I'd never fly with him."

Ultimately, it was the pilot's bullheaded personality that made him try to jam a sputtering plane (it had a rag in the fuel line), instead of patiently guiding it back to the airport—which a calm, even-tempered man could have done. Piloted by this ramrod of a man, the plane stalled and came down in a local tennis court. Jeff ruled the crash pilot error and said bitterly, "That man killed his whole family unnecessarily."

I learned about public safety versus airframe politics, and about the natural conflicts that arise between the FAA and the NTSB, two bureaus with wholly different philosophies. Jeff offered insights on human physiology and explained how you can tell, after a crash, who piloted a private plane . . . it's the person with two broken thumbs.

Most of all, I absorbed the esprit d'corps of the NTSB, the pride, the unwavering sense of duty, the abiding belief that what they do is one of the most important jobs on earth.

JEFF RICH GOT MARRIED while we were working together, and I went to his wedding. Unlike his colleagues, he found that one-in-a-thousand woman who loved him so devotedly she didn't care how often or how suddenly he had to rush off.

AS I RESEARCHED AND wrote, my critique group offered weekly doses of story insights, but now, added to their usual sharp critiques were occasional hopeful comments. "You know, Maralys, we think this book is going to make it. When you get *Scatterpath* published, it will drag *Higher Than Eagles* with it."

"You think so?" I said, and couldn't help feeling a fresh surge of optimism for the manuscript sitting in its orphan box, accompanied by little daydreams about my name in headlines and my writerly self seated next to some TV interviewer who is holding up books and carrying on about the author who sold two in one year.

MY CRITIQUE GROUP MAY have thought I'd embarked on a winning project, but my brother, Allan, did not. Now a grown-up version of the concerned and conscientious little boy who'd once tried to save me from my own ineptitude at Monopoly, Allan reacted with something akin to horror. Here was his own sister, offering the world's terrorists a recipe for bringing down airplanes. "You can't do this, Maralys," he said in all seriousness. "It's wrong. It's immoral."

"Not the way I've written it," I said. "The guy who really *could* sabotage planes already knows a thousand times more than I've put on paper. My book couldn't teach him a thing." I was smiling, thinking of the burden of morality my brother carries around like a suitcase you can never put down—the goodness that sometimes drives me nuts. "So what are the chances I'll reach some genius who's as gifted in computers as he is in airplane mechanics . . . and is also crazy to boot?"

"You said you were making your story real world," Allan said.

"Well . . . I guess I am. But only theoretical real world. My villain *could* exist. He *could* do all the things I've said. But I doubt we'll ever see that much brilliance and that much craziness in one person. So really, Allan, you don't have to worry."

"Hmmmm," he said, which probably meant I'd freed him up to go worry about something else.

WHEN THE BOOK WAS finished, I submitted the manuscript to every aeronautical expert I could find, from the past director of the Smithsonian Institution, to the chief test pilot for the B2 bomber, to a few private pilots, and even to one private pilot I knew rather well—our son Chris.

Chris took the pages without enthusiasm, which I assumed had to do with his being so busy doctoring people he had no time to doctor a book.

But that wasn't it. When he gave the manuscript back, a month later, he was smiling. "I didn't want to read this, you know, I figured you'd have a million mistakes that would drive me nuts. I was dreading it. Then I started reading, and it looked pretty clean. When I got to the end, I hadn't found a single error."

"You should trust me," I said.

"How could I, Mom? You're not a pilot."

"I know. But I had a pilot in my pocket."

"Well, he sure kept you on track. He must be a good teacher."

"Oh, he's very good. You'll meet him someday."

"No errors," he said again, shaking his head. "Hard to imagine I didn't find one. What are the odds?"

"Don't be so surprised, Chris. Nobody else found any either. Five aeronautical types besides you have read it, and the book came through without a change."

We stood at his front door, out of meaningful words, but not quite ready to part. "Sometimes," I said, feeling a sudden rush of gratitude for Jeff, "you just get really, really lucky."

*SCATTERPATH* BEGAN ITS JOURNEY to the outside world, an old, familiar trek that I'd long since stopped loving, that in fact was rather like a path to the guillotine. You send out your precious manuscript with hope and it comes back like an insult.

Most of the time nobody comments, nobody tells you what's wrong. They just send a form letter, or they type out a few trite words and turn it around. And you sit looking at the letter trying to find some shred of meaning, trying to read between lines that don't say anything, and you realize there's no meaning to be had in the words, "This isn't right for our house."

So you try to ignore your bad feelings, swallow them in a gulp, and tell yourself that that editor really doesn't matter, that he's wholly unimportant, which of course, since he didn't buy the book, he is.

And you brace to send it out a few more times.

EVENTUALLY YOU MUST HAVE an answer: What's wrong with this story?

I finally gave it to a friend, a man's man, the most masculine guy I know, so masculine and handsome, in fact, that he scares me. In the past, I'd found it nearly impossible to be coherent in his presence. When we're together, I talk to his wife and he talks to Rob.

But he reads a lot and he reads guy-type stories, and I imagined he'd have a clue about what was wrong.

He did. But it wasn't a criticism I expected. And I certainly didn't know at the time that his thoughts were critical, that they'd ultimately make that last, important difference . . . that this awesome hunk would end up saving my book.

## Chapter Twenty-Six

# WRITING FOR THE MALE MARKET

MY FRIEND, JOHN WALLACE, didn't take long reading my manuscript. As he handed it back, he said in his laconic style, "I can tell you what's wrong with it. It's too feminine."

He looked down at me in the impersonal manner of that familiar movie star who assessed women about like he might size up a favorite horse. Rob had always called him the corporate John Wayne.

Our John was tall, relatively laid back, and not in the habit of pouring out words, meaning you got only a few at a time. He was also one of the best-looking men I knew, which made my customary awe a decided handicap, because I really *wanted* to talk to this man. In the past, though, I'd never had any brilliant thoughts on things he cared about, like hunting or fly fishing . . . or about his job, either, as CEO for a major corporation.

Now we had something in common and it was infinitely easier to begin a conversation.

"So the book's too feminine," I said. "Oh, boy." Now wasn't *that* brilliant? "I wouldn't have known. Nobody's ever told me that before." On the spot I was trying to picture certain scenes and guess where the feminine taint might be . . . as though it lingered on the pages like a flowery perfume. "It's got to be a fixable problem—if I just knew where to start." I was thinking out loud, mumbling half to myself, hoping he'd be more specific.

"You want me to read it again?"

"Oh . . . " He was offering something that hadn't occurred to me. "Would you?"

He'd already done enough, but my reaction was spontaneous and heartfelt; no author could refuse such a gift.

"Sure. I can do that."

"Really?" I said. "To me, this is huge." And it was; I was truly overwhelmed. Our friend owed me nothing. But suddenly I was thinking fast. "Why don't we set up a code, then, to save you time. How about . . . "B" for boring, "W" for wordy, and "F" for feminine. Whatever you put on the manuscript will be better than what I have now, which is no clue at all." I thanked him, trying not to gush.

"Happy to do it," he said, and took the box away once more.

WHEN JOHN GAVE ME back the manuscript, I could hardly wait to be alone with it. Soon I was shuffling pages, on an Easter egg hunt for clues. To my surprise a first look revealed not many "B"s or "W"s, but pages that were littered with "F"s. He'd gone through it like a scientist on the prowl for bacteria, finding endless examples of diseased writing. Every third paragraph, it seemed, was all wrong for the male market.

Well. I certainly knew *now* where to start. At the beginning. In fact, he'd jotted on the very first paragraph: "This doesn't grab me. Not quite sure what is needed. Something is."

So there I was, with a finished manuscript that required a top-to-bottom makeover.

Some writers might have been discouraged, but I wasn't. It was so instructive, for once, to have something concrete to study and re-work, something beyond the vague, "This isn't right for our house." At last someone was telling me **why** this wasn't right for his house.

The more I looked through the pages, the more I felt John had missed his calling. As a second career, he could have been an editor for a major publisher. His analysis was sharp and specific, as finely-tuned as any words from an editor—from the best of my editors. He seemed to know **exactly** what I'd been doing wrong.

Between Jeff Rich and John Wallace I'd found two kinds of help, the kind for which any author would mortgage his soul.

John could see that I hadn't a clue about men—how they thought, how they talked, how they looked at life. As he pored over the pages, he seemed to get more and more exasperated with what he considered my spineless men, until on page 163 he finally wrote in a burst of words: "So far there is no strong character in this book. Wilcox (my hero) is weak, Brody (the boss) is weak, Halloway is really weak and Malec (the villain) has goats in his bedroom. Travis is also very shaky. Where is the hero? Not Knickerbocker? A good guy is needed—someone to identify with. In fact, at least two strong male characters are needed. Doubt if men will seriously take to a book where every man in it is weak, angry, or goofy."

Wow! His words were like a firecracker going off in my hand. You look down and you've lost your fingers.

I stared at that paragraph quite a while, thinking, Well, John, that's calling it like you see it.

It was one of those critiques you had to read over and over, not because you didn't get it, because God knows any idiot would grasp the message, but more to take the edge off, to blunt the points and make them less sharp. If you didn't finally get used to them, they were going to cut you until you bled.

So I read it quite a lot, and after a while that paragraph began to seem almost humorous. It had a ring to it, a cadence that sticks in your brain. He'd made his objections so clear that I found myself wishing I had his blunt, strong way with words. Bam. Bam. Bam. You knock 'em hard and knock 'em over. The way he'd written it, **he** was the strong hero every man looks for.

BECAUSE OF JOHN I had to re-think every paragraph. I kept trying to put myself in the head of a powerful man. I told myself, think masculine, think tough, think terse, think strong.

I began eavesdropping on men. Sure enough, they didn't talk like women. Whereas women never leave out a thing, articulating every word and every idea from beginning to end, men cut to the chase.

Their speech is abbreviated and choppy, with the core idea expressed but not much more. Men say things like, "Gotta go now." "Shoulda seen him—four hits in one game." "Can't do it today." "Shaq was a scoring machine—awesome."

Women would consider that conversational style the next thing to non-communication.

In places, John offered better word choices. Whereas I'd had a man say, "Let's leave now," he substituted, "Let's shove off."

He vetoed most of my cockpit conversations. "Pilots wouldn't talk like that. Too wordy." And where I'd written, "The pilots called in with fear-laden voices," he jotted in the margin, "Why knock the pilots?"

For that I had to call and ask what he meant.

"Pilots don't call in with fear-laden voices, for God's sake. Come on, Maralys, think about it. What kind of stuff do they find on those black boxes?"

Abruptly I knew. When a plane's going down you don't hear pilots moaning, "Oh dearie me, oh help, oh please, I'm so scared." Scared is not a word men even *think*. Or if they do, they don't express it. "Oh, shit," would top the list.

The more I thought about men and tried to play back their speech patterns and conjure up their thoughts, the more I understood. Emotionally, men are different from women; they translate most of their softer emotions into anger. A man who's scared usually curses. You make him sad and he still curses, but maybe under his breath.

In a few situations, I've asked my husband, "Weren't you scared?"

All these years he's never said yes. Instead he's said, "Well, I didn't like it much," or "I was plenty concerned," or, "You would have hated it." But admit he was scared?

Nah. Men are never scared.

Even the time Rob was on a plane that landed hard and blew out all its tires and skidded off the runway, he wouldn't use the Scared word. That time he said, "Well, it wasn't much fun. Sure I was worried. Flames were shooting out around the tires and I thought they might blow the fuel tank. You would have hated it, Babe."

So why hadn't I learned all this by listening to my husband? To my own five sons? Why didn't I get the idea years earlier? Who knows? I was probably too busy being a woman.

WHEREVER JOHN COULD, HE fine-tuned the male dialogue. Where I'd written, "Some busybody in Washington began playing big shot," John changed "Busybody" to "Asshole." Oh, yeah. Men don't talk like women.

In paragraph after paragraph, John truncated male dialogue, even inner thoughts. One of my characters said, "I noticed you eating alone. I could join you—that is, if you don't mind." John crossed out all that verbiage and wrote, "Mind if I join you?"

Not surprisingly, he went after the females, too. This was a man's book, and by golly, *everybody* had to be strong.

When it came to the one big sex scene, he wrote, "I'm no expert, but this comes across the way it would in a woman's book. It's too romantic."

I puzzled over that section quite awhile, unsure what to do. Never having known what transpires in a man's mind at such moments, I decided to head in another direction and go for humor. The humor seemed to work. No man ever faulted the sex scene again.

THE MAKEOVER TOOK WEEKS. By then I was reworking paragraphs besides those that John had marked; I was looking at everything. The words, Think Tough, Think Strong, Think Terse, rang in my head like a Catholic chant, like the beads on a rosary. I was also clenching my fist and tightening my jaw. No weakling was going to show his timid little face or speak his girlie pearlie words in my book.

With the manuscript bulked up like a linebacker on steroids, I mentioned to Patty Teal that I was once more ready to send it out.

She said, "I could try to sell it if you want."

"Would you, Patty?" We both knew she'd stopped being my agent long since, but at the moment I had no other.

Sure, she said.

We had a little discussion. I told her I'd done a few informal surveys as I gave speeches and found out, as most readers would guess, that while women will read men's books and do so all the time, few men will read a woman's book. "Look," I said, "I don't want male editors turning me down because I'm female. Let's send the book out as M.K. Wills."

Patty thought that was a good idea.

The manuscript only went out twice after that: the second editor bought it.

But even the first was gratifying in ways he never knew. After noting a few vague objections which, he said, kept him from making an offer, he ended his letter with words that rang in my head for years: "Please have Mr. Wills send me anything else he writes."

JUST FOR LAUGHS, HERE'S a story that goes the other way—about a man writing for the female market. A much-published author I knew well was inordinately proud that he'd written a romance novel from a woman's viewpoint—that he'd actually fooled an editor into thinking the author was a female. Yet it's hard to imagine a woman editor would ever be fooled by this man's prose.

Among other giveaways, from the heroine's viewpoint he'd written: "She knew her figure was wrong for gymnastics, but her tits were just right for cheerleading."

Chapter Twenty-Seven

# THE END OF A 14-YEAR DROUGHT

MY CRITIQUE GROUP DIDN'T get the sequence exactly right. *Scatterpath* didn't drag *Higher Than Eagles* anywhere.

Some time after I'd finished re-working *Scatterpath*, Rob and I were flying across the country when he happened to notice an article in TWA's *Ambassador Magazine*. The title read: **Small Presses Flex Big Muscles.**

He handed it across the arm rest. "Take a look at this, Babe. Might be just what you need." Rob's conversational style isn't exactly pure man's man, meaning he's not the brief-talker embodied by John Wallace, but he's close.

Well, nothing else had been much help lately, and with a *What the hell* attitude, I began reading. I was like a desperate overeater devouring diet books—never expecting miracles, but yearning for them just the same.

The article's logic was both scary and encouraging: as major publishers scooped up other major publishers and turned into powerful conglomerates, they focused almost exclusively on "big names"— best-selling authors, tabloid celebrities, and the occasional stunning writer who showed extraordinary promise—presumably because only those authors could guarantee a profit. Meanwhile, other talented artists, once known as mid-list writers, were rejected reflexively, with scarcely a second look. Now, the article said, small publishers were beginning to pick up the slack, among them not a few authors who later became literary award-winners.

Louis Rubin, founder of Algonquin Books of Chapel Hill, remarked in the article that he loves it when editors at big New York publishing houses ask him where he finds these remarkable talents. He must have smiled as he answered. "Most of those writers have already been turned down by New York."

The five small presses described in the article looked promising, and God knows *Eagles* had already been rejected by everyone big.

By then my memoir had taken on a life history not unlike *Schindler's List*. That story idea had been optioned several times by Hollywood, but when the movie was never made, the dedicated Jewish man who'd assumed the role of caretaker-of-history had tucked away his memorabilia in the back of his store and kept it safe. For years. Meanwhile, he ran a small luggage shop in Beverly Hills. It was sheer coincidence that the Australian writer, Thomas Keneally, happened to be standing outside the luggage shop on a hot summer day and that the proprietor invited him in to cool off. The two began talking about Schindler, and Keneally was fascinated. Eventually he wrote *Schindler's List*, the book that Steven Spielberg made into a movie. But none of that would have happened without the passionate Jewish man who kept the story alive.

By OCTOBER 1990, WHEN the TWA article was published, *Eagles* had disappeared from everyone's view, as though to the bottom of a lake, and nobody but me, and to a lesser degree, Rob, had even marked the spot where it went down. To the three agents who'd cared about it, the book's demise ranked as a sad commentary, a real shame, but nothing new in publishing.

By then I was almost finished with another book, *The Gatekeepers*, which was about a fraudulent HMO. (As far as I could tell, they were *all* fraudulent). Chris had allowed me to watch a hip-replacement— you see, authors **can** get into operating rooms—and I'd found a new agent who was trying to sell *Gatekeepers*.

Meanwhile, I'd sent copies of *Eagles* to all the small publishers listed in the *Ambassador* article. By now I was paying only loose attention to which copy was where, no longer mesmerized by the manuscript's every move as I'd been in its baby years. In fact, I'd become somewhat detached, aware that it might never sell and my passions would be better lavished on other books.

EARLY IN 1991, ABOUT midnight on a cold Saturday night, I went down to the mailbox to collect the day's forgotten mail. Among the junk was a small white envelope from Longstreet Press, about the size of a party invitation. I settled into my chair and stared at it with cold eyes—more annoyed than anything as I ripped open the envelope. *Just what I need, another rejection in the middle of the night.*

A check fell out. Mine. How curious, I thought, and began reading the stiff white card. The editor, Jane Hill, began by saying she was sending back my return postage. *The whole six dollars*, I thought wryly. Then she said, "I'm writing your agent to make an offer on your book, *Higher Than Eagles.*"

For a second I sat unmoving, stunned. I couldn't be reading this right. "Rob!" I cried, though he was sitting right there, three feet away. "You won't believe this. Listen!" And I read him the card.

"Well . . . that's good, isn't it?"

"Good? Is that all you can say? Good?"

I stared at him, waiting for more. His face hadn't changed; he was spectacularly unmoved.

I read the card again, scarcely believing it. In publishing, nobody ever, and I mean never, gives you that kind of news with a simple first-class stamp; it always comes via a long-distance phone call.

The moment became indelibly fixed in my mind. "Don't you realize what this means?" I cried. "This editor wants my book!"

He looked at me calmly.

But I wasn't calm, I was overwhelmed. Incredulous. The news had been so long in coming that my emotions ran outward in all directions, from disbelief, to joy, to a sense of vindication, to pride, to relief. "After all this time, they want *Eagles*! I can't believe it!" I jumped up and began dancing around the room. "After fourteen years!"

I couldn't help noticing as I carried on that Rob was a statue, that he was pleasant but subdued, and I'm not sure what I expected, that he'd jump up with me and do hand stands, I guess, match me scream for scream and arm wave for arm wave.

I should have realized that isn't Rob's style. He lets others do the emoting. In fact, the more hysteria swirls around him, the more he damps down.

Finally I yelled, "Rob! Aren't you happy? Don't you *care?*"

He paused, and his answer drifted back, distant and maddening. "I'll be happy when I see the check."

I just looked at him. Good God.


The next morning when I went out to play tennis, I felt as though I'd become an anointed person, that I literally glowed, elevated somehow to Pope-like stature. I expected my athlete friends to see this and respond with appropriate enthusiasm—with, at the very least, a desire to touch the hem of my skirt.

They did neither.

When I told them I'd sold my book, they said, "Oh, that's nice. We're glad for you, Maralys. Now who's going to serve first?"

To my astonishment, nothing more was said and the rest of our conversation revolved around *tennis.*

The match went by in a daze; for all I knew I was using the wrong end of the racket. Inside, I was thinking, "I've waited for this moment half my life! You guys don't get it. This is the biggest thing that's ever happened to me! It's fourteen years, now, it's a Nobel Prize. Can't you see, I'm a changed person!"

But they couldn't see; to them I was the same old me, a tennis friend they could laugh with who happened to sell another book. They'd never regard me as anything else. And finally I thought, *They liked you perfectly well before you sold the book, why should they like you any better now?*

But then it finally happened. I told my writing friends, and they all screamed and shrieked and carried on satisfactorily, and I thought, Thank God for the writers, because only they have the long-tortured psyches to grasp what this means.

SCATTERPATH SOLD IN 1992, the year *Eagles* hit the book stores. As it developed, neither book dragged the other anywhere, but none of that mattered anymore because I was happy enough to break out with two hardcover books in thirteen months.

THE NEXT CHAPTER IS about **Selling What You Write**, probably the topic my students care about most. When our class is discussing Agents and Editors and Query Letters and Near Misses, nobody ever interrupts to say, "Let's get back to our submissions." On this topic, they all want to hear every tidbit I have to offer, hoping that somewhere from my bag of tricks I'll produce the magic words that will catapult them into publication, money, and fame.

They don't hope as much as I do; I am with them all the way.

HIGHER THAN EAGLES DID fine. Better than fine. But only over the course of years would I see the myriad forms of excitement that can bubble up from a once-orphaned, now oft-celebrated book.

Chapter Twenty-Eight

# SELLING WHAT YOU WRITE

MY STUDENTS ARE DEVOTED to this topic. We're all devoted to it. And why wouldn't we be? Selling is the culmination of the endless, painstaking work we've done over so many years. It's the *purpose* of all that effort. It's the reason we strive so hard at first to make our work better, and ultimately it lies behind our mad, crazy push to reach a higher plateau and burnish our words until they shine. Selling is everything.

*If your work is good enough, it will sell.*

I've always believed this. But only for me, and people like me. I know about my insane personality, about having the voice of the *Reader's Digest* ringing in my head, about getting rejected and thinking immediately, with gritted teeth, *I'm going to make this better. I'll make it so good they'll **have** to buy it. I'll show you!*

As much as I'd like to see all my students develop insane personalities, it's obvious that many won't, that even some who write beautifully won't see the need for obsession when it comes to selling.

Published authors are apt to say that all of us need "luck," and that luck favors the prepared. True enough. But obsession is what takes you to the place where luck happens.

SELLING WHAT YOU WRITE has two components, irrevocably linked: superior writing and bull-headed determination. Without an unwavering willingness to do whatever it takes, we'd never accept the truth: if our work isn't selling, it's probably not good enough.

But when you finally know for certain it **is** good enough—when even your own words make you tingle inside and leave you kind of breathless and wanting to read on—you can safely assume it hasn't sold because you haven't tried hard enough. You haven't gone that last mile. Maybe you haven't gone that last hundred miles.

My students may dislike hearing that I have no magic keys, but only a magic attitude; they're doubtless wishing for more. But attitude is the best I can offer, an immutable, positive, forge-ahead attitude . . . combined with unshakeable images of oneself as published.

OKAY, SO YOU HAVE the book and you have the attitude . . . what's next?

Everything starts with a query letter. Single-spaced, one page, so the agent will read the whole thing in one quick sitting.

Query letters, like first pages, are tricky little beggars and hard to get right, almost impossible to get exactly right. The tone is critical. The writer must sound confident but not braggadocio, she has to give information but also create story questions, she has to capture the spirit of a book while keeping the letter brief.

Query letters contain four vital sections: an introductory "**Hook**," a brief **Summary** of the book including its category (two or three paragraphs); a few sentences describing the author and her **Credentials**; an **Offer To Send Chapters** (or the entire book). Bang. Bang. Bang. Should be a breeze.

It's anything but.

Still, there are places to get help. Try reading book jackets. Read the inside flaps. Editors know how to write "selling" copy, and their techniques are on display in every book in the bookstore. With practice, you can imitate the tone, the vivid words, the brevity. It's all right there.

As an example, here's the inside flap of *Scatterpath*. If my query letter had been that good, I'd have doubtless sold the book sooner:

"The freak accidents keep happening—crashes and near crashes, on-board computers going haywire—but only on Airtech aircraft, and only on its new "fly-by-wire" planes. Is it a faulty design in software, pilot error, or something far more sinister?

Investigations of black boxes and analysis of computer programs turn up nothing. Only Air Safety Investigator Alan Wilcox, operating on gut instinct, senses the ominous truth—someone, somewhere, is sabotaging these airplanes. In the face of massive disbelief by his colleagues, in danger of sacrificing a family that is coming apart at the seams, one lone safety inspector takes on the aviation community, the FAA, and the National Transportation Safety Board, searching for pieces of the diabolical puzzle."

There's more, but in a query letter, these two paragraphs would have done it.

Unpublished authors find the "author-credential" lines daunting. They shouldn't. If your book covers a topic in which you're an expert, say so. ("I worked ten years as a nurse . . . a lawyer . . . a marine biologist.") You can mention taking writing courses for however many years, the longer the better, anything to prove you're determined and have a professional attitude. Remember, agents love to "discover" new talent.

The query letter that eventually sold my book, *Higher Than Eagles,* was later re-printed in the 1992 *Writer's Market.* A bit of luck—that it was *my editor* the reference compilers happened to call. They wanted a query letter that sold a book, and she sent them mine. Students have asked to see the letter, so here it is:

Dear Miss Hill:

The excellent article in TWA's *Ambassador* magazine, "Small Presses Flex Big Muscles," gave new hope to all of us who've written midlist books and have heard the gloomy and oft-repeated statement, "The midlist is dead."

By coincidence, *Crazy Ladie* is one of the books I brought home from the ABA. It is a wonderful, literary story—beautifully written, all the characters so vivid!

The manuscript I'm writing you about is a nonfiction called *Higher Than Eagles,* the story of my son, a hang gliding champion, who overcomes a difficult childhood to accomplish everything he set out to do in life. Though he died at twenty-six, we realized later it might not be the length of a man's life that matters so much, but whether he lived life very well.

The story contrasts the difficult, early years of a stubborn, single-minded boy beset by asthma, with his years of triumph, when he became the U.S., Canadian, and British hang gliding champion. He is the flyer who did all the hang gliding sequences in the Smithsonian Institution's epic, *To Fly,* and he was the subject of a *Sports Illustrated* article on hang gliding. Though the book focuses on my oldest son, Bobby, it is a family story told by me and my second son, Chris.

My credits include six published books: four category fiction and two nonfiction. *Manbirds: Hang Gliders and Hang Gliding* (Prentice-Hall, 1981), was listed by Library Journal as one of the 100 best in Science & Technology and *Fun Games for Great Parties* (Price/Stern/Sloan, 1988), went into an immediate second printing.

If you'd like to see *Higher Than Eagles*, the manuscript is ready to send.

Sincerely,

A last caution, especially for men: be careful about writing query letters that come on too strong, that sound like a Madison Avenue sales pitch. The cocky, hard sell, smart ass approach that works in business doesn't work with agents. They hate it. Agent friends have shown me those letters—always from guys—and the agent goes from being turned off to laughing behind the sender's back.

Here are two recent letters that brought no results but a few chuckles from an agent. The first was one of dozens that arrived in a virtual shower from different parts of the country, all supposedly from "friends" of the author: "Hi, Agent X. What foresight—grab a hot, young author like Sam Everyman and you're set for decades! Jim."

A second author made his pitch via an attorney: "Dear Agent X. We would like you to represent a $20,000,000.00 book project and would like to know your percentage.

"We will only discuss the matter with you and/or our attorneys **if you are interested**.

"We have heard that you may be an excellent agent for California and or/the USA rights. Sincerely,"

An agent at a conference laughed derisively over the query letter that advised her to " . . . take my manuscript and a cup of coffee and go sit under a tree and enjoy yourself."

An author need see only one such reaction to swear off the Madison Avenue approach forever.

So WHERE DOES AN author send his polished query letter?

Agents are your best bet; few major publishers will even consider unagented material. Agent listings can be found on the internet, in the library's LMP (Literary Market Place—the only exhaustive list) or in such reference books as *Writers' Market* and *Jeff Herman's Guide to Book Publishers, Editors, and Literary Agents.*

The last two, which don't include every possible agent, do contain crucial information about those they list. The agents are pretty honest. They describe what kinds of books they're looking for, their agency's submission requirements (a chapter, for instance, or several chapters), their willingness to look at unpublished writers, their response times (never as short as they say). With this information the author can save himself significant effort. No point in sending science fiction to an agent who specializes in romance.

It's fortunate so many agents now ask for sample pages or sample chapters; it takes pressure off the query letter. If an agent fails to specify, *always send the First Chapter.* That's the one that counts. (See Chapter on Beginnings)

BESIDES THE ABOVE REFERENCE books, smart authors find potential agents and editors another way: they haunt the bookstores and locate published books that are somewhat like theirs and search inside for the Acknowledgements page. Almost every savvy author will thank the editor and agent who helped produce the book, and you can presume those agents would at least take a look at other, similar books.

IF YOU'RE AS DOGGED about getting published as you need to be, you'll go to writer's conferences—as many as you can. Here you'll meet editors and agents face to face, which gives you a better sense of them, and they of you. For some conferences you're invited to submit pages of your work to be critiqued. (Which costs extra, of course.) National conferences are listed in LMP.

I was lucky enough to be taken on by an agent I met at the Maui conference. But even had I never found an agent or editor anywhere, every conference I've been to has offered excitement, inspiration, and earth-solid information.

We writers come home all pumped-up, full of zest for what we're doing, more determined than ever to get to our computers and write that fabulous book. Conferences are invariably positive, predictably full of people like us who love books, love the process, love to share what they know.

It's possible to do everything right, and still have no chance of selling. The book that fits no recognizable category, that isn't aimed at any particular set of readers, that can't be placed in any of the well-known sections of the book store, is probably a lost puppy.

Publishing is all about marketing, and if an agent has no idea who on earth will buy your book, she won't take it on.

GETTING PUBLISHED IS HARD, it's always been hard, but it's not impossible. Think of Pearl Buck, who really did send her books on a slow boat from China . . . and Dr. Seuss, who might never have been published if he'd been walking, one critical day, on the wrong side of a New York Street.

Think of all the well-known authors who endured years, literally years, of rejection. But kept going anyway.

Every published author has her story of what it took, that first time, to get published.

I doubt, though, that many can describe half a dozen first times, which is how an author is punished for being a genre hopper. When you're forever working in a new category, you're also constantly knocking on new editorial doors, poking your head in and saying, "It's me!"

when nobody inside has the foggiest notion of who "me" is.

DRIVEN ALWAYS BY ATTITUDE, the following are some of the steps I've taken to get published.

My first published book, *Manbirds: Hang Gliders and Hang Gliding*, came about because I listened to my agent friend, Patty Teal, and sent an editor a telegram, offering to write a book for him—different from the one he'd already rejected. The details are covered in Chapters Eleven and Thirteen.

The romances came next, the only easy sells of the lot—at least the first three. It was agent/friend Patty Teal again who suggested I try this new genre, and Patty who quickly sold three books with no help from me. The fourth, a romance centered on hang gliding, was a different matter. No matter how hard she tried, or how many new versions Betty-Jo and I submitted, that book remained stubbornly unsold.

Then one day an important editor came to our RWA meeting and said she was looking for action/adventure books. I stared at Debra Matucci from Harlequin American, hardly believing what I'd heard, that an editor actually wanted the very book we'd been trying to sell. At the end I rushed up to her, and Matucci suggested I send her a proposal, and I did—a brand-new outline for what had become a much-rejected theme. I knew when Betty-Jo and I wrote it that this was the best version yet, and wasn't too surprised when Matucci quickly sent Patty the contract.

SELLING NEVER CAME EASY again.

Chapter Twenty-One describes the seemingly-endless process of trying to sell *Fun Games for Great Parties*—of sending out *a hundred-and-thirty-seven* query letters—an unreasonable effort, since who in his right mind would imagine the 138th publisher might buy what 137 others had rejected?

On the other hand, who will ever work as hard for you as you'll work for yourself?

And that's one of the points to be made here: as authors, even agented authors, we often have to get involved in the selling process, to offer ideas or help with footwork.

Ultimately, the party game book sold when I contacted Price/ Stern/Sloan for the second time and made an appointment to meet the Vice President in person.

After the failure of three different agents to sell *Higher Than Eagles,* that book seemed doomed. But having sent it myself to yet another, one-last-publisher, I sold it at last to Longstreet Press.

Until *Scatterpath* underwent the John Wallace transformation, I was its agent, and God knows how many times I mailed it out. All to no avail.

After its face lift, Patty took on *Scatterpath* and sold it quickly. But when I didn't like the editor's offer, she let me talk to him myself. It was an interesting negotiation, because I thought so little of the advance he was offering, I really didn't care whether he bought the manuscript. The editor knew I was dealing from strength and finally asked that memorable question, "What would it take to make you happy?"

I wished later I'd asked for double the amount; I think I might have gotten it.

Among my most recent selling efforts was a public policy book, *Save My Son.* Though I had an excellent new agent by then, the one I'd met at Maui, she endured several months of frustration until I finally urged her to try a publisher I'd run across numerous times as I did research. That, of course, was the house that ultimately bought the book.

Nine published books, then, all agented. Yet I was instrumental in selling five out of nine. In fact, I can honestly say, without my efforts, those five might never have sold at all.

None of this can be construed as bragging. God knows, there's no pride to be found in having to put dynamite under your work to sell it.

WHEN IT CAME TO my tenth book, a light-hearted memoir that my agent didn't stand a chance, I decided not to spend another fourteen years trying to beat down the walls that sealed off most conventional publishers. I made a conscious decision to try self-publishing. But I also sought out the best publisher of this type in the business—Ivy House Publishing Group—and was rewarded with a book that evoked the word Quality and appeared as polished as any of the trade paperbacks in the bookstore. When *A Circus Without Elephants* won an award in the *Writer's Digest* International Self-Published Books contest, it was a triumph (and a lovely surprise), that propelled me into the sale of two more books—this time with Stephens Press in Nevada.

Stephens Press published not only the sequel, *A Clown in the Trunk*, but this book on writing.

Which brings me to one more step a writer can take in her attempt to sell a manuscript: Whatever it takes, try to get a positive review from a well-known author.

Knowing Sidney Sheldon would speak at a writer's luncheon, I brought along a manuscript for this book, hoping against hope I might speak to him personally and persuade him to review it.

The letter in its entirety reproduced on the next page, describes what happened.

NOT EVERY BOOK IS worth saving. Four of mine lie unfinished or unsold, some because a window of public interest closed before I'd perfected the manuscript, others because I lost interest.

Of the books I cared about passionately which, to me, had too much merit to abandon, I eventually sold them all.

And perhaps this is the final point to be made about selling: If you believe your material is good, right up there with other selling books, you should never, absolutely never give up, either on the polishing end or the marketing end. With an attitude like that, you'll sell most of what you write.

# Sidney Sheldon

PALM SPRINGS, CALIFORNIA 92262

Dear Maralys,

When I found your manuscript packed in the bag I brought home from the Roundtable West luncheon a few weeks back, I knew there was not a snowball's chance in hell that I'd have time to read it. I was not only in the process of doing a final edit on my memoir, *The Other Side of Me*, but my wife and I were (and still are) in the midst of moving out of a home which has been my residence for nearly four decades – a task which is far more daunting than either one of us had ever anticipated.

As I sat at my desk, thinking about the letter I would dictate to my assistant to inform you of my dilemma, I found myself almost mystically drawn to your manuscript. As I read, each sentence compelled me to read the next, and before long I was completely lost in your wonderful book. So it is with great pleasure I offer you the following endorsement:

*Maralys Wills, genre-hopper extraordinaire, will make you laugh and cry and laugh again in this gripping how-to handbook for writers everywhere. She is clearly a force to be reckoned with.*

My heartfelt congratulations to you on a job well done, and best wishes for a smashing hit book.

Warm regards,

## Chapter Twenty-Nine

# SAVE MY SON

It was six years before I sold another book, though I was writing as diligently as before.

When you're a writer, you write. It doesn't matter whether you sell or not (well, yes, it does matter), but not selling doesn't mean the process stops, it doesn't mean there's no creating, it simply means you write with a tighter jaw and a greater sense that time is slipping away.

Once hooked, you can't stop. The Force takes you by the hand and drags you off to the computer and sits you down to do your thing. And all the time you're thinking, if you happen to be an incurable optimist, *By damn, this book will sell.*

But sometimes you have to face the fact that you've finished a book that nobody will buy in its present state. So you re-do it entirely, and then discover nobody will buy it in its redone state, either, and you're asking yourself, *How much obsession should I commit to this manuscript*? How much fretting, how much starting over? Eventually the pages drift into a pile on the nearest chair and soon the pile gets stashed in a file cabinet, and when you discover it years later, you can no longer remember the names of the characters.

Such was the fate of *The Gatekeepers.* A good story, I thought, and so did quite a few readers, including some respected doctors, but after years elapsed (with the only benefit being a fascinating research/lunch in the U.S. Senate dining room), **everyone** was aware that HMOs were semi-fraudulent. The story wasn't hot anymore. It wasn't even lukewarm.

Rob kept saying, "You didn't get that book out fast enough, Babe, while HMO's were still big news. You should have jumped on it, taken advantage of all the controversy."

I just looked at him. Where had he been? Hadn't he noticed all the jumping I'd been doing the past three years?

"God, Rob, I was writing like a maniac. Practically obsessing. But it takes an editor to jump in with you."

And I'd never found one. The rest of the world didn't care that my topic was fast solidifying, like cold Cream of Wheat. As authors, I thought, we can only write and re-write, we can only try to find agents, and the agents can only try to find publishers, and beyond that, you can't wrestle an editor to the ground and force her to take your book.

Which brings up an important caution for new writers: Don't try to capitalize on the country's latest Hot Topic. By the time you find a publisher it won't be hot anymore.

By the late '90s, I was once more looking for a project. By coincidence a respected surgeon asked me to co-author a book on breast cancer. He was so enthusiastic that he swept me into his vision. The doctor was a remarkable man and so were his patients. I'd already begun the research, a few touching interviews with some very brave women . . . when I paused to search the web for competing books.

Amazon.com stopped me cold. I sat there staring at the screen in dismay. Here were *hundreds* of books on breast cancer, some so highly touted it seemed unlikely we'd ever be bought.

Pushing ahead with hopeless books no longer seemed even slightly appealing, and I told the surgeon regretfully that writing a book, even *desperately wanting* to write a book wasn't enough. You had to believe, at least minimally, that you could sell it.

We both let it drop.

AS HAPPENED SO OFTEN, my next project was unlike any I'd tackled before.

For years our youngest son, Kirk, had battled alcohol and drug addiction. Still, I never lost my long-range vision of him . . . our son standing tall and bathed in light because he'd recovered miraculously. I'd see myself writing a triumphant story. The book would be unflinching in its worst details, but would end with heraldic trumpets. "If our son can shake his addictions," I'd say proudly at the end, "anyone can."

But first his problems had to be solved. Nobody wants to read a book that's negative from beginning to end.

The years went by and Kirk never improved.

Instead, his dealings with the criminal justice system (with prisons, to be truthful), had changed and hardened him, so that now, besides addiction problems, he had personality problems.

By the late '90s it was obvious I was never going to write a book about Kirk. There was simply nothing useful or positive to say.

ALL THAT CHANGED WHEN a friend suggested I meet Mike Carona, an Orange County Marshall then running for Sheriff. "He's got ideas you need to hear," said my friend, Nancy Clark. "Let me tell him about you and what a fine writer you are."

Which is how Mike Carona and I happened to meet for breakfast one morning at Mimi's restaurant.

He was a trim man with a military bearing and strong features. We sat across from each other, staring at the menu.

With the breakfast ordered, I plunged right in. "Nancy Clark says you've got some unique ideas for hard core drug addicts."

He smiled. "Well there's one solution, anyway, which I may or may not get to try." He told me about his plans for lock-down drug facilities. Instead of ordinary, punitive jail, a non-violent addict would be offered treatment in a minimum security facility, where he had no choices and for once couldn't just walk away.

I said, "That's the first workable solution I've heard in years. It's a wonder it's not being tried everywhere."

"It is being tried in a few prisons—but no jails. If I'm allowed to start such a program in Orange County, it'll be the first in-jail program in the country."

My enthusiasm grew. For addicts like Kirk, this could be an answer. "For years," I said, "we've sent our son to voluntary programs that haven't worked. When he gets bored with people probing into his psyche, or fed up with all the blabbing—as he sees it—he just leaves."

He nodded. "That's always been one of the failings of non-coercive treatment."

The two of us exchanged thoughts on the futility of the criminal justice system and how it's done almost nothing to curb the country's addiction problems but has, in fact, done a great deal of real harm.

"Look, Mike," I said suddenly as the idea came to me, "how would you like to help me write a book? We could be co-authors."

I caught him off guard. He looked at me intently. I could almost see the wheels turning. "What kind of book were you thinking about?"

"Well, about your ideas, mainly. About the criminal justice system and its failures. About solutions for the drug problem." My thoughts enlarged as I spoke. "You realize you can't lose. If you're elected sheriff, you can put your plan into practice. If not, at least you'll have a book out there." (Why do I go on blurting things like that? As though selling a book is automatic?)

He smiled. "Okay," he said. "I can go for that." And right there in the restaurant over scrambled eggs, with a simple handshake, we began a partnership that would go on until the book was finished.

MIKE'S HOURS WERE CONSUMED with running for Sheriff. For me, it was time to begin working.

Thinking I might get an early commitment for our book, I went to a writer's conference in San Diego and talked to a few editors, all of whom frowned and took on the dubious expression of someone being offered a book on sewage treatment. One added, not unkindly, "That would be a hard book to sell."

I nodded and thanked him. Of course it would be a hard book to sell. *All* books are hard books to sell.

Toward the end of the conference, I was standing at the top of a stairway when the title for the book rushed into my head, as though it had whooshed up the stairs. *Save My Son*, I thought. Perfect.

OUR PROPOSAL, NEARLY A hundred carefully worked (probably over-worked), pages, went off to my new agent, Barbara Braun. She was enthusiastic; all we needed now was an editor.

For a while it seemed there was no such editor.

One cannot help feeling compassion for agents, who send out proposals with great enthusiasm and high hopes, only to see them crash against glass walls, like the birds who keep hitting our picture window. You have to feel a tad sorry, too, for all the editors whose hands are tied, especially those who were once free to make decisions based on their own gut reactions.

I have **no** sympathy for CEOs who run publishing companies but don't read books.

EVENTUALLY, WHEN IT STRUCK home that half my preliminary research had taken place in books published by Hazelden, Barbara Braun approached the Minnesota company, and soon two editors came to California to meet Mike and me.

Our dinner meeting at the posh Nieuport 17 seemed to go well, and I called Mike later. "What do you think, will Steve Lehman buy our book?"

"My guess is, he will."

MIKE CARONA BECAME SHERIFF and we sold our book almost simultaneously. Though he'd suddenly become the busiest man I knew, he still returned phone calls and promised to do his part.

"This can't be a regional book," I said to my new editor, Steve Lehman. "It has to be national. I'll have to visit other states, find out what they're doing about addiction."

Lehman agreed.

I knew instantly where I'd go: any state where I had a friend or a relative. Virginia was the home of my lawyer son, Kenny . . . Colorado had long been home to a close college friend . . . and Arizona was the most forward-looking state, treatment-wise, in the country.

The word research took on new luster. In various states I visited detention centers, drug courts, prisons, diversion centers, jails, and therapeutic communities. Research left me feeling exhilarated. How had I once been so ignorant? Until then I'd never heard the term therapeutic community. I knew nothing about drug courts. It's a wonder I'd heard of prisons.

Best of all, I met the extraordinary people who ran these institutions—most of them not merely dedicated, but passionate. As one warden of a Virginia diversion center said, "You have to have a fire in your belly."

RESEARCH. IN THE COURSE of a few books I'd gone from avoidance and scorn to uncontained enthusiasm. I'd become an author who'd just as soon spend her days absorbing events, places, and personalities as crafting sentences. I'd become, God forbid ... a researcher.

MIKE AND I WROTE separate personal chapters: his was about his mother, whom he discovered dead of alcoholism when he was eleven: mine was about our family's twenty-year struggle with Kirk.

As we began analyzing the results of our research (Mike also sent out teams of men), we could see that whatever California's criminal justice system was doing for addicts, it wasn't working. Our mission was to point to policies that *did* work, to enlist the power of all those people with a fire in their bellies ... the judges, DAs, and lawmakers.

The two of us had only to meet a few accomplishing, grateful, recovering addicts to know that trying better methods was worth the effort.

By year's end, we had a manuscript ready to send to Steve Lehman. With relief, I delivered it to the post office; I imagined our project was over.

It wasn't.

Instead of the compliment-laden phone call I expected, Lehman said distantly that we'd have to discuss a few problems in January, and he kept us wondering through the holidays what those problems might be.

Once again I'd finished a book that wasn't finished. I seem to specialize in such attempts, I'm the author whose trademark is twice-written books.

Which means, considering the horrendous waste of time and paper, I can only come out on top if readers appreciate them twice as much.

Chapter Thirty

# THE VOICE OF GOD

AFTER THE HOLIDAYS, OUR editor, Steve Lehman, called to
explain what was wrong with *Save My Son*.

At first I was baffled. "I'm not sure what you mean."

"Well," he said, "you have to get yourself, the author, out of the
middle. The chapters which aren't about you and Kirk, or about Mike
and his mother, have to be impersonal, with a ring of authority."

"Oh," I said, and suddenly his message came through in capital
letters. "The book has to resonate with the voice of God."

"Something like that."

He wasn't as sure as I was, but that *was* what he meant. Figuratively,
a lofty presence had to preside over the text with a cool voice and a
dispassionate attitude. Nobody as trivial as an author could intrude
on the authoritative statements from experts. The "I" word had to
disappear, and people who were interviewed could not be responding
to a questioner, they had to be speaking from an unseen podium.

I did get it.

The job wasn't as hard as I imagined; it was an easy assignment,
going through the pages one by one and taking out me and substitut-
ing God.

In no time at all I was finished.

Steve Lehman liked the new version and once again the manuscript was finished.

How were we to know that a militant copy-editor, the man-hater from hell, would come along soon afterwards and try to destroy it?

COPY-EDITING IS SUPPOSED TO be a once-over-lightly job, a last look at the manuscript for spelling and grammar errors, a rooting out of factual inconsistencies. The copy editor's job is to catch small mistakes—like the character who sports blue eyes in one chapter and brown in another.

Copy editors do not, as a rule, render opinions on content.

But ours did.

As a courtesy, publishers send authors the copy-edited version for one last review, and until *Save My Son*, no copy-editor had ever posed a problem; like most authors, I was simply grateful that someone had caught those final few errors.

Inexplicably, we'd drawn a copy editor with an agenda. This one marched across our pages determined that all females be given equal treatment to males. She began by changing half of all the impersonal "He" pronouns to "She", and half the "Him"s to "Her"s. On some pages she made changes in alternating paragraphs, assuring a state of bedlam for any reader trying to follow the text.

By the third chapter, it was obvious to me what she was doing. I called Steve Lehman, trying not to whine, but whining anyway. "She's ruining the book, Steve. It's reading like crap."

"It's your book," he said. "Change whatever you don't like." So I began applying the word "Stet," a proofreader's term that means "leave as is," working feverishly to blot out her presence.

It got worse. In an ever more militant mood, she crossed out physical descriptions of females, claiming we hadn't described any males, which in fact wasn't true.

She went ballistic when we noted that women have a gentler approach to encounter groups than men, that they giggle more and curse less. She lined that out and wrote in the margins, "Suggest you omit this. Insulting to women."

Did she really think it nobler for women to behave like furious males and curse like stevedores?

By now my irritation had risen to new heights and every negative feminist stereotype became part of my mental image, and I could almost see her . . . and she certainly wasn't anyone I'd want to know.

I went on stetting, though not indiscriminately. First it meant looking hard, two or three times, at what she'd done, on the off chance she was right about something— though mostly she wasn't. She had no better sense of writing style and rhythms than she had about the basic, obvious inequality of the sexes.

The process was maddening and took forever—a couple of weeks— to get her angry presence out of our book.

Had Mike and I accepted her changes, I doubt that a single reader would have persisted past the first few chapters.

*SAVE MY SON* CAME out in late 2000, and for nearly a year, Mike and I were written about in newspapers and appeared together on radio shows and on television. After all our efforts, that was the part I reveled in, the radio talks, the press, the cameras, the speeches . . . the dessert.

Letters came to us from grateful mothers, mostly those with sons in the same sorry state as Kirk.

Neither of us can claim we've saved the world. But we suspect we've changed more than a few minds about the best approach to America's drug problems.

[Author's note: Mike Carona has since become embroiled in criminal proceedings, none of which I could see coming. His program for lock-down drug treatment did prove to be effective.]

AFTER A YEAR SPENT promoting *Save My Son,* I was once more without a project . . . unthinkable for a writer, rather like being without food. For most of us, it isn't a matter of *wanting* to write, or *hoping* to write, it's simply that we **must** write. Getting up in the morning with no job waiting in the wings would be intolerable.

Not sure which of many projects should come next, I began work on a book that had beckoned to me distantly for years . . . a compilation of all the stories composed for what Rob and I call our *Annual Report.*

Our *Annual Report* is not just about me. Rob writes a serious philosophical essay, plus he compiles an eight-page section of carefully-selected family photos. I focus on the highlights—the year's events that strike me as comic or dramatic. Most are humorous. Or at least they're meant to be humorous.

With this book I tried to be funny. I gave funny my all . . . stretching, reaching, re-writing. Once again I'd genre-hopped into a new field.

The next chapter is all about humor—what little I know. As any humorist will admit, humor is not easily defined, or even described. Humor is just "there." It's either present in your work or it isn't. And if you've captured it, I defy you to tell anyone exactly how it was done.

## Chapter Thirty-One

# WRITING HUMOR

OF ALL THE GENRES I've tackled, humor is near the top in degree of difficulty. Since few of us can define exactly what humor **is**, fewer still can tell you how to do it. One of my best students said to me in all seriousness, "Early in my career, I read a whole book on the craft of writing humor. By the end, I didn't know any more about the subject than I'd known at the beginning. The author didn't know how to write it, either."

This chapter might be easier if all of us could agree on what's funny. But we can't. And here's an example of why not. In one of my recent stories sent to our Christmas list, I described two horrific falls taken that year by my husband and me. Mine came first: as I left an unlit tennis court after dark, I fell, more like flew, over a mammoth rock—while nearby, my husband merrily rode past on a golf cart, sweetly unaware that the whole family was yelling at him to stop.

A month later, just as his granddaughter's volleyball game was starting, my husband caught his foot on something at the fourth tier of the bleachers and came catapulting down the steps and finally splatted all over the gymnasium floor. He survived, of course, and after the game, a friend remarked, "I do believe, Rob, you got more court time than some of our players."

A few of our readers penned notes expressing genuine sympathy, while others said things like, "I yelled at my husband to come here and read this, and I was laughing so hard I could hardly speak."

So there you have one of the problems. We all laugh at different things.

In fact, trying to tell someone how to write humor is on par with defining a void. We can skirt around the edges, but our best attempts will merely point to what it **isn't**.

ANGER IS NEVER FUNNY. Study the work of any well-known humorist—Dave Barry, Erma Bombeck, Bill Bryson, David Sedaris, Betty McDonald, Mary Roach, and you'll never find any of the characters becoming flat-out furious. Frustrated, yes. Exasperated, maybe. Bewildered. Perplexed. Put-upon. Harried. Confused. But they never cross the line into genuine anger, because comedy writers have all figured out that's where humor evaporates like mist.

When somebody's *really mad*, all of a sudden you stop laughing. Even the Marx Brothers and that low-comedy team, The Three Stooges, never seemed genuinely angry, in spite of considerable footage devoted to one or another using planks to bop the others over the head.

TALK OF LAUGHTER ISN'T funny. Like the stand-up comic who has to keep a straight face, the stand-up writer must appear to be serious. The moment you write about people laughing, the humor inexplicably seeps away. It's like telling your reader, "Here's where you laugh." And then they don't.

AN ENTIRE BOOK DEVOTED to humor stops being funny. After a while the reader wearies of the author's non-stop attempts to make him laugh. The reader longs for a respite, for something serious he can hang onto. I've never personally read a book of unalleviated humor that didn't eventually become boring.

Conversely, some of the best humor stems from tragic situations. Two examples come to mind: As most of you know, we lost two sons in hang gliding accidents. After Bobby's death, I was given the job of choosing a casket—now for the second time. With Bobby's widow,

Suzette, and one of his friends, I wandered, dispirited, through a funeral home trying to make a choice. Suddenly it all seemed so empty. So pointless. "What does it matter what casket we choose?" I said. "None of this will bring him back."

Unexpectedly, Bobby's friend said, "Maybe we should try Rent-A-Casket."

Right there in the funeral home, the three of us exploded. We laughed so hard, so uncontrollably, that we had to leave. None of us will ever forget the black humor that had relieved our grief for a moment.

The other example is from *Dancing in my Nightgown,* Betty Auchard's book on widowhood. She describes a husband who'd been a great spouse—except for his compulsion to tell her how to drive. When after his death, she was driving home with her husband's ashes on the passenger seat, she said, "It was the first time I'd ever been in the driver's seat when he wasn't telling me what to do."

Most good playwrights, like Neil Simon, know that humor is at its best when mixed with pathos.

THE BEST HUMOR DEPENDS on a moment of surprise, or an event the reader didn't quite see coming, and it's that reflexive element of seriousness-gone-awry that strikes people as funny. Often it's a matter of somebody providing an inappropriate response to an unexpected occurrence . . . as in that famous one-liner: "Besides that, Mrs. Lincoln, how did you like the show?"

The need for surprise creates extra problems for the writer. After he's struggled to make a scene funny, the author himself is no longer surprised, even slightly, and his perspective on the humor, or lack of it, dims with each re-reading, until his best work seems to have all the vitality of a crippled mouse.

No writer needs a critique group more than the humorist. On the other hand, judging humor is so dismayingly subjective, that the comedy writer needs bunches of critique groups, because in at least half, the work will be read by someone who over-inflects and drives the comedy off the page.

How you deliver a comedic line is everything. It's an art so subtle that it can't be described: it's a matter of how you breathe, how your voice rises and falls, how you pause, and even the look on your face. I've discovered I can be funny giving speeches to crowds, especially when I throw out little offhanded zingers; but I almost never get laughs in small groups—especially if I'm so careless as to announce in advance, "Let me tell you this funny story." I've arrived at the end of one of those stories and found everyone just looking at me. Not a smile anywhere. And there's also this sticky tension hanging over the group, usually created by the sound of one person laughing. Me.

So be prepared for your funniest written scenes to fall like a soufflé under the inept inflections of a bad reader. Most of all, you need a reader who isn't *trying* to be funny; if laughter comes spontaneously from the others, you know the words are good.

A HUMOROUS SCENE NEEDS what is known as "call back." You set up an incident with numerous funny elements, and you re-visit one of them at the end. Example: my son wrote a story about the time he "crashed" a formal event at the Savoy Hotel in England. By bluffing outrageously, and in spite of the fact he was wearing jeans and his date a housedress (with everyone else in long gowns and tuxedoes), he persuaded the hostess to seat him down front, "displacing two diplomats from Tunisia, who were suddenly at the wrong table." The two disgruntled diplomats were moved to a table in the rear. The preposterous evening is described at length. At the end of the story, there's a mention of the photographs still in the archives of the hotel. In their portrait, my son and his date are smiling serenely, while nearby we see a photo of "two scowling diplomats from Tunisia."

As a humorist, you quickly learn that some words are just naturally funny, and you become adept at picking them out of a lineup. You also discover that formal, "stuffy" writing can go a long way toward building humor (or kill it altogether.)

Having just written two books that depend almost entirely on comic situations, I still find the craft of writing humor as elusive and uncertain as it was in the beginning. The process is hopelessly vague. I "fiddle" with my scenes. I try things, discard them, and start over. Later, in the act of re-reading the work, I tweak the writing some more ... always on the prowl for better, funnier words. I go back and play up scantily-described settings, or enlarge on the characters' attitudes. I try to tap into frustration, exasperation. I search actively for additional, funny details. For instance, when my husband catapulted into the gymnasium, coins fell out of his pocket and began rolling across the wooden floor. Three men rushed to pick up my husband. My daughter rushed to gather up the money. (When I describe this scene to others in front of my daughter, who has a great sense of humor, she does not think it's funny.)

The struggle is worth it. Writing good humor has one of the most satisfying payoffs in the business. Nothing sings in a writer's heart quite like the sound of readers laughing.

I must have succeeded in my first book-length attempt at humor, because (as you now know,) my memoir, *A Circus Without Elephants*, won that national award from *Writer's Digest*.

Chapter Thirty-Two

# THE PAYOFF

NOW, AFTER TWELVE PUBLISHED books and four that weren't, a question mark shimmers on the horizon: why am I still doing this?

Why, when I'm Maralys Wills to a few scattered editors but simply "Who?" to all others ... when my writing income is about a nickel an hour ... when no university is clamoring to drape me in purple and make me its commencement speaker ... why do I keep opening up new screens on my computer and typing Chapter One?

I suppose it's all a matter of self-image, of knowing who you are.

I am a writer.

I write because the compulsion to do so flows through my psyche like the blood through my veins, because I consider any other occupation (for me), a waste of a good life. Because any lengthy, non-creative interval makes me feel like a hamster on a wheel.

I am most alive when I'm writing. Everything else I do, which includes being with friends and family and giving them time (never begrudged, never consciously truncated), is a kind of exhilarating tune-up to the hours I will soon spend crafting sentences. I live my life with the thought that sooner or later I'll get to the dessert. To my book. There's no particular hurry; I will arrive there eventually, because all these hours my body's been leaning like a wind-blown cypress in the direction of my computer.

Without a literary-list to one's body, there is scant reality to the oft-heard declaration, "I'm going to write a book someday"—though people say this with a gleam in their eyes, as if the book will magically happen one day when they're not looking.

You realize nobody ever says, "I'm going to write a symphony some day." For those who intend to write a symphony, music has become so engrained in their souls they could not excise it if they wished to. And that's how it is with words. For the writer who *will* write a book, words have become so entwined with his inner being that the writing itself is just a natural extension of a love affair already begun.

For me, for an author who has blurred her career with too many interests and too much genre-hopping, I can only guess that the books written so far won't make me a "name" in American letters. Yet I'm still unable to look back and decide that here, with this book, or there, with that one, I should have stopped and built a career.

I just wrote what I wanted to write. And I never quite believed that you can't construct a house by laying brick foundations on six different lots.

It's all wrong, and nobody will argue that it isn't. But think what I've learned! Think of all the nuances gleaned about different genres, think of the accumulated wisdom that will benefit my students.

Think of *this book*! Among all my books, this treatise was the most fun to write. A gift for me and a present for my writing students, whom I adore.

Which brings me to a final thought: while writing, to a writer, is surely the highest and most glorious use of one's time, sharing what you've learned with other aspiring writers is right there on the same elevated rung.

For all you avid authors out there, struggling as I've struggled, I can only hope that this books helps you capture your own story, that it inspires you to do what we've all had to do—keep on keeping on.

As a teacher, and an author telling a story, I try to save the best for last. The best in my writing career was what happened after

*Higher Than Eagles* was published. Looking back at fourteen years of re-writes, of ever bigger envelopes to hold ever more rejections, of alternately giving up and pushing on, I'd have to say it was like struggling across endless dusty plains in a covered wagon, never sure you or the wagon will make it, then climbing the Rockies and after that the Sierra Nevada mountain range and coming down the other side to find oneself gazing across a sweet, gentle land toward the Pacific Ocean.

The excitement, the relief, the clasping to one's chest of this concrete object you've wanted so long would have been enough. But there was more.

Writers like columnist Jack Smith and author Elizabeth Forsyth Hailey offered stunning comments for the book jacket.

Reviewers in *Publishers Weekly, Kirkus, and Library Journal* all gave the book fine critiques, better than I might have dreamed.

The *Los Angeles Times* ran a very large, illustrated story on the book, later reprinted across the country in fifty-two newspapers.

*20/20*, the television newsmagazine, sent an interviewer to our home for an entire day with the thought of doing a national story.

The book was optioned for the movies five times. Two of the options were from Finnegan-Pinchuk, the producers of *Northern Exposure*, and Walt Disney Productions.

People wrote incredible letters about how they'd stayed up all night to finish the book, or read it in a weekend, or loaned it to five other people—so many letters, in fact, that they had to be moved into a larger envelope.

WITH ALL THE YEARS that have intervened since the publication of *Higher Than Eagles,* it's safe to say that the repercussions have never stopped coming. Even today, I am stopped by readers in banks and stores who have read the book and passed it on to others and want several more copies for friends.

I am the Jewish man in the luggage shop, holding on to a vision and never expecting a miracle to happen, but hoping it might just the same.

The ultimate payoff, the best gift of all, would be a full-length feature movie, with Bobby and Eric coming to life once more on the screen . . . to live again as they lived in my mind and on my pages for fourteen years.

Though I dare not expect it, surely, surely, it is still all right to dream.

The End